# London Assurance

The success of Ronald Eyre's new production of *London Assurance*, presented by the Royal Shakespeare Company in the summer of 1970, reintroduces to the English theatre a comedy first staged in 1841 which was an established favourite for fifty years but which had not been staged since 1913. Ronald Eyre's achievement, by means of a sparkling production and telling adaptations to the text, was to eliminate the difficulties and elements of raggedness from this lively and subtle play, written before the author was twenty-one, and to allow its considerable comic qualities to shine through.

This new edition makes available to the reader both Boucicault's full original text and the text of Ronald Eyre's modern acting version.

*The photograph on the front cover shows Judi Dench and Donald Sinden in a scene from The Royal Shakespeare Company's production in 1970 and is reproduced by courtesy of Patrick Eagar. The portait on the back cover is by F. D'Avignon and shows Dion Boucicault in 1855. It is reproduced by courtesy of Christopher Calthrop and the Theatre Collection of the Harvard College Library.*

# Methuen's Theatre Classics

THE TROJAN WOMEN Euripides
*an English version by Neil Curry*

THE REDEMPTION *adapted by Gordon Honeycombe from five cycles of Mystery Plays*

THE MISANTHROPE Molière
*translated by Richard Wilbur*

LADY PRECIOUS STREAM *adapted by S. I. Hsuing from a sequence of traditional Chinese plays*

IRONHAND Goethe
*adapted by John Arden*

THE GOVERNMENT INSPECTOR Gogol
*an English version by Edward O. Marsh and Jeremy Brooks*

DANTON'S DEATH Buechner
*an English version by James Maxwell*

BRAND Ibsen
HEDDA GABLER *translated by Michael*
THE WILD DUCK *Meyer*
THE MASTER BUILDER
MISS JULIE Strindberg
*translated by Michael Meyer*

THE IMPORTANCE OF BEING EARNEST Wilde
LADY WINDERMERE'S FAN
THE UBU PLAYS Jarry
*translated by Cyril Connolly and Simon Watson Taylor*

THE PLAYBOY OF THE WESTERN WORLD Synge

# DION BOUCICAULT
# LONDON ASSURANCE

*The full original text*

*Adapted for the modern stage and edited by*
RONALD EYRE

*with an introduction by*
PETER THOMSON

METHUEN & CO LTD
11 NEW FETTER LANE LONDON EC4

*The original text of* London Assurance *first published in 1841*
*Ronald Eyre's new stage adaptation first published by*
*Methuen & Co Ltd 1971*
*Copyright © 1971 by Ronald Eyre*

SBN 416 63310 2 (*hardback*)
SBN 416 63320 x (*paperback*)

*Printed in Great Britain by*
*Cox & Wyman Ltd.,*
*Fakenham, Norfolk*

# Contents

DIONYSIUS LARDNER BOUCICAULT: BIOGRAPHICAL NOTE    vii

INTRODUCTION *by Peter Thomson*    viii

EDITOR'S INTRODUCTION    viv

AUTHOR'S PREFACE TO FIRST EDITION (1841)    xx

CAST LIST    xxiii

LONDON ASSURANCE    1

# Dionysius Lardner Boucicault

26 December
|      |                                                                                                     |
|------|-----------------------------------------------------------------------------------------------------|
| 1820 | Born in Dublin. |
| 1830 | Moved to London with Dionysius Lardner to continue schooling. |
| 1836 | At the University of London, studying Civil Engineering. (Boucicault's own claim.) |
| 1838 | Joined provincial company (Cheltenham) as an actor. (Took stage name of Lee Moreton.) Played leading comic role in his first professionally performed play, *A Legend of the Devil's Dyke*. |

4 March *London Assurance* opened at Covent Garden,
1841 under the management of Madame Vestris and Charles Mathews.

1843 The monopoly of the legitimate drama by the Patent Theatres (Drury Lane and Covent Garden) abolished by Act of Parliament.

1844 To France in search of plays to adapt for English audiences.

1845 Married French lady, who may have died in a fall in the Swiss Alps.

1848 Returned to London with several plays ready.

1849 *The Willow Copse* (from the French) a success at the Adelphi.

1851 Associated as writer and actor with Charles Kean's company at the Princess's Theatre.

1852 *The Corsican Brothers* and *The Vampire* staged by Kean.

1853 Quarrelled with Kean and eloped to America with Kean's ward, Agnes Robertson. Worked in American theatre with his wife.

1857 *The Poor of New York* staged in New York.

1860 *The Colleen Bawn* staged in New York. Returned to London to arrange staging at the Adelphi.

| 1864 | Provincial opening of *Arrah-na-Pogue* (Dublin). |
| 1872 | Returned to work in American theatres. |
| 1874 | *The Shaughraun* staged in New York. |
| 1882 | Lectured on 'The Art of Acting' at the London Lyceum. |
| 1885 | Eloped to Australia with Louise Thorndyke, whom he considered his wife. |
| 1888 | Appointed a teacher in school of acting at Madison Square Theatre. |
| 18 September 1890 | Died in New York. |

# Introduction

Dion Boucicault was born in Dublin on Boxing Day, 1820. His mother, Anne, was the sister of the poet and playwright, George Darley. His father may have been Samuel Smith Boursiquot, whom Anne Darley married in 1813, but was more probably Dr Dionysius Lardner, encyclopaedist and popularizer of scientific knowledge, after whom Boucicault was named and who became his guardian. Boucicault's sketchy education began in Dublin, continued after 1830 in London, and may have ended with a year at the University of London as a student of civil engineering. By this time he was writing dramatic sketches and planning a life in the theatre. In 1838 he joined a provincial stock company (at the Theatre Royal, Cheltenham), using the stage name Lee Moreton. For most of the rest of his life the careers of actor and dramatist were twinned. He was the lead comic in his first professionally performed play (*A Legend of the Devil's Dyke* at the Theatre Royal, Brighton in 1838), and the lead comic still, at the age of sixty, when he played the acrobatic title role of *The Shaughraun* in Dublin in 1881. *London Assurance* was the second of his plays to be presented in London. It opened at the Theatre Royal, Covent Garden on March 4, 1841 and received the unusually high number of sixty-nine performances that season. Boucicault was paid £300 for the manuscript, less than the £100 per act offered to established dramatists, but a windfall for a beginner. His subsequent attempts at comedy, plays like *The Irish Heiress* (1842), *A Lover by Proxy* (1842),

*Alma Mater* (1842), *Old Heads and Young Hearts* (1844) and *The School for Scheming* (1847), failed firmly to establish his reputation or his earning capacity. London managers found it both safer and cheaper to commission adaptations from successful French plays than to bring out English plays. Always an opportunist, Boucicault went to France in 1844 to trap possible plots at source. He stayed there until 1848, inevitably impressed by the Parisian taste for farce and for historical melodrama. His first marriage was an uncertain mixture of melodrama and farce. The story, far from verifiable, was that his French wife had a title, a modest bank balance, and twice his years behind her. They honeymooned in the Swiss Alps, where the lady fell, leaving Boucicault her money and a widower. On his return to England, he cashed in on his knowledge of French plays, notably with *The Willow Copse* at the Adelphi in 1849 and with a sequence of sentimental 'cape and sword' melodramas written for Charles Kean, whose memorable decade as manager of the Princess's Theatre began in 1850. The most important of the 'Kean' plays were *The Corsican Brothers* (1852) and *Louis XI* (1855), both very much 'from the French'. During fifty years as an active dramatist, Boucicault wrote, adapted or concocted about 200 stage-pieces, a number which includes farces, pantomimes, musical interludes and operettas, but after 1852 melodrama was his favoured mode.

The useful relationship with Charles Kean was short-lived. There was a quarrel, and Boucicault left for America in 1853 with a new wife, Charles Kean's ward and the leading *ingenue* of the Princess company, Agnes Robertson. For several seasons husband and wife acted in New York and on the road, whilst Boucicault gauged the taste of American audiences. The demand, he decided, was for 'the actual, the contemporaneous, the photographic'. The plays written between 1857 and his return to England in 1860 are fine examples of his mature style. Credible relationships, sketched in speakable dialogue, are threatened by villainy and disaster. Pathos is a powerful component, and there is always the theatrical magic of a 'sensation scene', Boucicault's most vivid contribution to melodramatic style. The first piece of this kind was *The Poor of New York* (1857), mutated for touring purposes into *The Poor of Liverpool*, *The Streets of London* and *The Streets of Dublin* (1864): the best, and a superb example of its author's theatrical resourcefulness, was *Jessie Brown*; or *The Relief of Lucknow* (1858): the most 'contemporaneous' was *The Octoroon* (1859), which took slavery in the southern states as its theme and had its villain unmasked by a camera. It was New York that staged the opening night of *The Colleen Bawn* (1860), the first of the three Irish melodramas by which Boucicault is now best remembered. It was probably the success of this play that persuaded him that the time had come for a return to England. He took the script to Benjamin Webster, manager of the Adelphi, with whom he made an historic agreement – to share the risk by sharing the profits instead of receiving a down-payment for the manuscript. It was the first time dramatist and manager had entered into such a partnership, the condition of the later wealth of writers like Henry Arthur Jones, Pinero and Barrie and one of the means by which greater talents were tempted back to the theatre. Boucicault's own position was vastly improved. For the next few years, mainly in London, he could indulge his well-known taste for good living. Sir Squire Bancroft could remember dining with him as a young actor in his house at Earl's Court, where the star item on a long wine-list was a 'Cognac, 1803' from the cellars of Napoleon III, which 'had the imperial "N" on the bottle'. In *The Colleen Bawn*, *Arrah-na-Pogue* (1864) and *The Shaughraun* (1874), Boucicault provided himself with his best acting parts, comic Irishmen who combined an inventive indulgence in blarney with an off-hand heroism in the service of that great melodramatic virtue, loyalty. These are by no means his only Irish plays, but the verdict of posterity that they are the best is probably a fair one.

From 1873 onwards most of Boucicault's dramatic work originated in the U.S.A. In 1876 he set up home in New York, where he continued to spend more money even when he began to make less. *The Shaughraun* itself is said to have brought him over half a million dollars, but it is uncertain how much of his fortune remained in 1885, when he suddenly left Agnes Robertson and bigamously eloped to Australia with Louise Thorndyke, an actress not much older than the eldest of his five children. This was not the first of Boucicault's affairs. The young man who, in 1841, had greatly increased the importance of Lady Gay Spanker in *London Assurance* because of his infatuation for Mrs Nisbett who was to play the part, did not settle easily into the bourgeois marriage for which his wife was better fitted. There was a notorious 'incident' with a Mrs Jordan in 1862, and other relationships can be discerned between the lines of recorded biography. But the 1885 elopement was un-characteristically shabby. Boucicault even tried to claim that his common-law marriage to Agnes Robertson was not binding. For over thirty years she had been his companion on the stage. Now she divorced him. His third wife seems to have been genuinely loving, but his last years were not easy. Plays did not flow from his pen as they used to, money was scarce and he was too old to act. He tried journalism, and late in 1888 became a teacher at a recently established school of acting in New York. According to Daniel Frohman, he was drafting new plays and scheming new schemes just a few days before his death in September, 1890.

The eighteenth-century theatre had tried rigidly to separate the 'kinds' of drama from each other – and failed. The nineteenth-century theatre increasingly abandoned the attempt, settling for plays which mingled song, anguish, laughter and spectacle or anything else that would help them to 'go'. The only certain, rigid distinction was that between 'legitimate' and 'illegitimate' drama, and that was more a matter of law than of aesthetics. The Letters Patent issued by Charles II had given the control in London of the legitimate drama to Thomas Killigrew and William D'Avenant, and to their heirs and assigns. When Boucicault began his career the patents were still in force, settled now on the two houses of Drury Lane and Covent Garden, with a limited 'summer' licence available to the Haymarket Theatre. The illegitimate houses were restricted, in law at least, to the performance of plays with music, though the tricks used to evade the full rigour of the regulations were more numerous than the informers employed by the Patent Theatres to expose them. One of the most enterprising of the minor houses during Boucicault's apprenticeship was the Olympic Theatre in Wych Street, managed from 1830–39 by Madame Vestris and, after their marriage in 1835, by Charles Mathews as well. Particularly in the fairy plays and extravaganzas of J. R. Planché, they developed a style of comic underplaying which introduced 'real' behaviour into designedly fantastic plots and settings. In 1839, ambitious and already in debt, they bought their way into the management of Covent Garden, determined that their careful productions should be seen in one of the legitimate drama's two homes. The move was mistimed. The power of the patents was on the wane – in 1843 they were abrogated by act of parliament – and both Drury Lane and Covent Garden were experiencing hard times. The Vestris management had a series of disasters in the 1840–41 season, and *London Assurance* was a desperate last hope. It was staged in the closest thing London had yet seen to a box set, and there is no doubt that public interest in this scenic innovation contributed to the piece's success. The play just failed to save the Vestris management, but it did young Boucicault a power of good.

There is something oddly anachronistic about *London Assurance*. Its dramatic ancestry is of the eighteenth century – Farquhar, Goldsmith, Arthur Murphy – and, despite its popularity, it had scarcely any progeny. By 1841 the five-act comedy, and anything in less than five acts was to the purist *no comedy*, was no longer a flourishing form. 1840 had seen the first performance of Bulwer-Lytton's *Money*, an accomplished piece with a profoundly Victorian subject and a dissonantly eighteenth-century formality in treating it, but there were few other notably successful 'classical' comedies written in the previous twenty years, and fewer to follow before the crucial appearance of Tom Robertson's *Society* in 1865. Between *London Assurance*, the outstanding example of the mid-century's attempt to keep alive the comedy of wit, and *The Importance of Being Earnest* (1895), there is nothing of stature to prepare the theatrical way for the later play. Tom Robertson's comedies are not witty, W. S. Gilbert's witty plays are not comedies, and the work of H. J. Byron and the later punsters is despoiled by witticisms. Wilde renewed an interest that dramatists like Henry Arthur Jones (*The Liars*, 1897) and Pinero (*The Gay Lord Quex*, 1899) would have liked to sustain. Jones and Pinero were more original, or at least less plagiaristic, than Boucicault, but less talented too. It is, perhaps, a pity that Boucicault's sensitivity to public demand led him away from comedy, although the defection added greatly to the more characteristic Victorian mode of melodrama. That the move was a conscious one, and that Boucicault set out to preserve the comic spirit in his melodramas, is evidenced in a letter he wrote to the Bancrofts shortly before Robertson's death in 1871:

The public pretend they want pure comedy; this is not so. What they want is domestic drama, treated with broad comedy character. A sentimental, pathetic play, comically rendered, such as Ours, Caste, Colleen Bawn, Arrah-na-Pogue.

Robertson differs from me, not fundamentally, but scenically; his action takes place in lodgings or drawing-rooms – mine has a more romantic scope.

Robertson and Boucicault are the two greatest names in mid-nineteenth-century drama, both pre-eminently men of the theatre, expert in stage mechanics and stage management, and using that expertise simply to entertain and incidentally to instruct; because that was the tradition of theatre that they knew, and that was the way to keep the money coming – just.

PETER THOMSON

*Manchester, October, 1970*

# Editor's Introduction

It was my good fortune to read *London Assurance* as one might read a new play – without prior knowledge of the author and before the press notices. Shaw, I learned afterwards, had consigned it to a particular limbo for plays which are so dead that they do not even date ['. . . if "London Assurance" were revived (and I beg that nothing of the kind be attempted) there would be no more question of dating about it than about the plays of Garrick or Tobin or Mrs Centlivre']. The editor of the O.U.P. *Nineteenth Century Plays* called it 'a comedy of manners palely reminiscent of Congreve'. Eric Bentley included it in his anthology, *The Development of English Drama* (Appleton-Century-Crofts) but gave it a sour little testimonial: '"London Assurance" is good entertainment for an unthinking audience.'

The play was handed to me with a proposed cast-list and a request from the Royal Shakespeare Company to read it more as a blue-print for an evening in the theatre than as a sacred text. Its appeal was immediate: warmth, prodigality of comic invention, vigorous dramatic language and parts to fit an unusually gifted company of comedians. To the question 'What is it about?' which faces any director and needs an answer before he can get to work, the answer came along these lines: it is about good feeling, what sustains it, what kills it, where to find it, how to lose it. It is the story of four love-affairs: the love-affair of Grace and Charles, the conventional meeting of the prettiest; the love-affair of Pert and Jenks, the conventional meeting of the most business-like; the love-affair of Mr Spanker and Lady Gay, the astounding meeting of the least likely; and the love-affair of Sir Harcourt Courtly and his mirror. This desolate Narcissus straddles the play, excluding and excluded, none the wiser and none the happier for his experiences – simply older. His is the posture of emptiness.

Though I would stand by that as a nutshell account of Boucicault's play, it is rather more concealed than apparent in the original text. And much tactful and some savage rewriting and drawing-out were necessary before it started to show. Here, in more detail, is the reasoning behind the changes and the shape they took.

*Structure*

1. Sir Harcourt meets his Waterloo when he elopes with Lady Gay. Until he makes that decision he is, though ripe for a fall, unendangered and the play up to that point is a series of comic exposures of the London beau under a variety of rural pressures. By the time the elopement is planned, Act Four is well advanced and Boucicault leaves himself only Act Five for the elopement, the exposure and the general dénouement and restoration of good will. Though no one would willingly sacrifice the desultory comedy of the earlier acts, the elopement plot does start late and is dispatched perfunctorily. Those critics who complained of a falling-off in the latter part of the play may have been equally unsatisfied if the dramatic style of the first three acts had continued till the end, making of the play a protracted mosaic documentary of country peace disturbed by urban intruders (and presumably ending with Grace Harkaway married to Sir Harcourt Courtly).

The changes in this part of the RSC version are twofold. The first half of Act Five is played as an exterior. This does ventilate the action which otherwise takes place in a succession of rooms. At the same time the text here has been cut and reshaped. I cannot help thinking, though, that if the audience could stand the elaboration, there's a case for extending the elopement still further – to some remoter site perhaps. With freer staging than that at the Aldwych and a bold pen some such expansion could justify itself.

2. Mr Solomon Isaacs, though mentioned by name in Act One does not appear till Act Five. In the revised version the end of Act One is reshaped to introduce Isaacs in person and to put pressure on Charles and Dazzle to make a quick getaway.

3. In the latter part of Act Five where a duel is expected, Boucicault, in an understandable nervousness at the amount of explanation and reconciliation to be gone through before the curtain falls, allows news of the impending duel to be followed by the entry of Sir Harcourt and an immediate explanation of why it never took place. In the RSC version the resolution of the duelling is drawn out and Spanker is given a scene in which he

can reach his full angry height, thus making it less eccentric of Lady Gay to devote herself to him.

## Continuity of Characters

In the original, Pert is introduced, given her head and dispatched in one Act only – Act Two. She is mentioned once more but is otherwise unused for the rest of the play. Jenks, her intended, is named but never appears. Meddle departs, deflated and spare after the duel.

In the revised version Jenks appears as full-time attorney and part-time fiddler and, as Pert shows herself to be an adequate pianist, they are used to supply music for the ball that Max gives his guests. Once allowed as musicians, they have a right to be involved in the rest of the action and at the end, when one lawyer is needed to manage the legal transaction of paying off Mr Isaacs, Max has the choice of two – Jenks and Meddle – and, as the choice goes, Meddle's fortunes dip and Jenks's rise.

Meddle's presence in that last scene is another addition: he now appears with Mr Isaacs at the end of the play. In the original, Isaacs was spared the benefits of legal aid.

## Language

There are moments of intentional parody (e.g. Grace's florid speeches in Act Three) not to be confused with a sort of deadly fine writing (e.g. in the first meeting of Charles and Grace in Act Two). Where this latter occurs, cuts are made [] or other lines substituted.

Some verbal changes that may seem finicky (12), (44), (99) were suggested by a first manuscript draft of the play which is in the possession of the playwright's great-grandson, Mr Christopher Calthrop, who generously put at our disposal his fine collection of Boucicault material.

In its earlier form, *London Assurance* was called *Out of Town* and is of more than passing interest in this context.

## Out of Town

In this early draft Sir Harcourt was called Sir William Dazzle. (There is one residual 'Sir William' in the printed text in a speech of Cool in Act One.) His son was Charles Dazzle whose alias, Augustus Hamilton, was Jack Scatter.

The Dazzle of *London Assurance* is an anglicization of Ignatius Mulvather, an Irish adventurer, and the character loses something in the transfer. Take, for instance, Mulvather speaking to Lady Gay about duelling: 'Matters of this kind are indigenous to my nature as an Irishman independently of their pervading fascination to all humanity.' The equivalent speech in *London Assurance* omits the phrase 'as an Irishman' and thereby loses its anchor. The discovery that Dazzle was a misplaced Irishman led to rehearsal experiments at the RSC in which first the actor concerned, then other members of the cast, put on Irish accents. Oak Hall certainly made new sense as a place in which a lawyer could be mistaken for a gardener, a neighbouring landowner could be overlooked standing abstracted on a staircase, a squire could suddenly decide to have a ball. Even when English accents were resumed, something of Irish inconsequence remained – to the play's advantage.

At the time Boucicault's manuscript came to hand a decision had already been taken in rehearsal that Grace Harkaway should be played as a blue-stocking, as little at home in the country as in the town and only really at home in a book. Welcome confirmation of this view of Grace came from rejected dialogue in *Out of Town*. In that part of Act Two where Charles regrets there is no opera within twenty miles, Grace goes on:

'You speak Italian, of course?'

'Oh, like a native,' he replies. So she speaks to him in Italian. He shifts to French, his vernacular. She shifts too and he cannot answer her. He considers Greek, Spanish and Hindoo before he opts for a more direct love-game. Later, indoors, the subject of music arises.

GRACE. Mr Scatter, are you a musician?

CHARLES. Not at all, madam. (*Aside.*) No more bragging. My Italian and French cuts are still sore.

*Spanker*

Though Grace Harkaway in the RSC production is an unusual romantic heroine – bespectacled, bookish, censorious, daunting, as if Boucicault were quizzing Charlotte Brontë – the characterization has confirmation in *Out of Town*. Adolphus Spanker, on the other hand, is handled by the RSC in a way Boucicault would not own. Spanker, as Boucicault sees him, is timid. He stammers, tears his glove in his anxiety at meeting Sir Harcourt, is trapped into suspecting his wife and duelling for her. His decisions are made for him. Yet this is the man who inspires Lady Gay Spanker (by universal consent a 'devilish fine woman') into a tender admission of deep love. For her sake there should be steel somewhere in Spanker.

For her sake then Spanker was played in the RSC production as a man not so much afraid as abstracted. The main note given to the actor was to think of himself much involved with bee-keeping or a butterfly collection and more interested in the contemplation of that than in small talk at the squire's. The dashes in his early speeches, instead of being a stammer reaching a block and a gulp, are tokens of a man's mind taking off on thoughts more congenial than the conversation around him. And while he thinks, his companions have to await his return.

Spanker can be played in this way to spectacular effect in his first scene. And it is not inconsistent that such a man, after burgundy and brandy-punch, should strike a vein of rotund fluency. But from his subsequent scene with Meddle onwards, when the drink has worn off, there has to be some return to the man who arrived with silences in Act Three. Boucicault's words do not allow it. In a future production, and with the assurance of knowing how well the early Spanker worked at the RSC there would be a case for editing Spanker's speeches in his later scenes to make them fit his earlier.

### Staging and scene divisions

Boucicault demands five settings: a house in Belgrave Square, the exterior of Oak Hall and three of its interiors. The RSC version used three settings: Belgrave Square, the exterior of Oak Hall and one interior. The scene-changes used a revolve. The main scene-piece was the exterior revolving to the interior of Oak Hall. Belgrave Square was an inset in the Oak Hall interior. The Acts were renamed. Acts One, Two and Three of Boucicault became Act One, Scenes one, two and three at the RSC. Then came the interval. Act Four became Act Two, Scene one, Act Five was split to make Act Two, Scenes two and three. In the RSC version Act Two, Scenes one and three were the same interior as Act One, Scene three. Act Two, Scene two was a night version of the same exterior as Act One, Scene two.

### The Text

The text used and reproduced here in full is the 1841 published version. The cuts made in the RSC version are indicated by square brackets in the text. The alterations and additions are indicated at the foot of the page, under the main text. The

extension of Charles's speech in Act Three (beginning of [96]
follows Lacy's Acting edition (1851), as does the revised scene
order for Lady Gay's first scene. The dramatic advantage of
Lacy over the earlier version in this instance is that it throws
Lady Gay's long description of the steeple-chase to the end of
the sequence. This gives Sir Harcourt an increasing opportunity
of studying the lady in action – first her appearance, then her
small-talk, leaving till last the bracing evidence of her skill in the
saddle.

RONALD EYRE.

*October, 1970*

To

CHARLES KEMBLE

this comedy

(*with his kind permission*)

is dedicated

*by*

*his fervent admirer and humble servant*

DION L. BOUCICAULT

AUTHOR'S PREFACE TO FIRST EDITION (1841)

There is a species of literary modesty observed by authors of the present day – I mean, that of prefacing their works with an apology for taking the liberty of inflicting them upon the patient public. Many require no such plea; but the following pages are too full of flagrant faults to pass from me without some few words of extenuation.

The Management of Covent Garden Theatre requested me to write a comedy – a modern comedy; I feared that I was unequal to the task; but, by the encouragement and kindness of Mr CHARLES MATHEWS, I was induced to attempt it. Once begun, the necessity of excessive rapidity became evident; and, on the spur of the moment, I completed this work in thirty days. I had no time to revise or correct – the ink was scarcely dry before it was in the theatre and accepted. I am aware that it possesses all the many faults, incongruities and excrescences of a hastily-written performance. It will not bear analysis as a literary production. In fact, my sole object was to throw together a few scenes of a dramatic nature; and, therefore, I studied the stage rather than the moral effect. I attempted to instil a pungency into the dialogue, and to procure vivid tones by a strong anti-thesis of character. The moral which I intended to convey is expressed in the last speech of the comedy; but as I wrote 'currente calamo' I have doubtless through the play strayed far wide of my original intent.

Let me take this opportunity of stating the facts attending my reception at Covent Garden Theatre – as it may also hold out encouragement to the faint hearts of many entering the perilous shoals of dramatic literature.

In the beginning of last November I entered this establishment under the assumed name of LEE MORETON. I was wholly unknown to any person therein. I received every mark of kindness and attention on the part of the Management and was cordially welcomed on all sides; my productions were read without loss of time; and the rapidity with which this play was produced – together with the unsparing liberality of its appointments – give ample proof that the field is open to all comers.

*London Assurance* was made to order, on the shortest possible notice. I could have wished that my first appearance before the public had not been in this out-of-breath style; but I saw my opportunity at hand – I knew how important it was not to neglect the chance of production; the door was open – I had a run for it – and here I am.

How shall I return thanks adequate to the general sympathy and hearty good-will I have received at the hands of the mass of talent congregated in this piece.

MR W. FARREN'S personation of *Sir Harcourt*, made me regret that I had not the part to rewrite; the *ci-devant jeune homme* – the veteran *roué* – consummate vanity – blunt, lively perception, redolent with the very essence of etiquette – the exquisite – the vane of the *beau monde*, – were consummated in his appearance; before a word was uttered, he more than shared the creation of the character.

MR HARLEY in *Meddle*, was, as Mr Harley is universally acknowledged to be – irresistible.

Who could view the quiet, deliberate impertinence – the barefaced impudence of *Dazzle*, reflected in MATHEWS, without the reiterated roars of laughter which attended nearly every word he uttered – passages which I never intended as hits, were loaded, primed and pointed, with an effect as unexpected to me as it was pleasing.

MR BARTLEY as *Max*, gave a tone and feeling to the country squire, both fresh and natural. To this gentleman I am under the greatest obligation for the numerous and valuable suggestions which he tendered; and to him I must attribute to a great extent, the success of the piece.

I have to offer my most sincere thanks to MR ANDERSON, for the kind manner in which he accepted the part of *Courtly*; the prominence which it held in the representation, was wholly attributable to his excellent impersonation.

What can I say to MR KEELEY; praise would be superfluous; his part had one fault in his hands: it was not long enough. [*Mem.* To correct that another time.]

Out of the trivial character of *Cool*, MR BRINDAL produced effects wholly unexpected. Let him not imagine, that by mentioning him last, I prize him least.

MRS NISBETT did not enact – she was *Lady Gay Spanker* – the substance of my thoughts; she wore the character with grace and ease, divesting it of any coarseness, yet enjoying all its freedom. She dashed in like a flash of lightning, and was greeted with a thunder of applause. What can I say of this laughing, frolic creature? – Has Momus a wife? If he has not, let him make haste.

MRS HUMBY, with her usual good-nature, undertook a very paltry page or two, grinding blunt humour into the keenest edge, with a power which she alone possesses.

To those who have witnessed this play, I need not describe my gratitude to MRS C. MATHEWS; to those who have not seen it, I must express my inability of expression. I am well aware, that to her judgement, taste, and valuable suggestions, with regard to the alterations of character, situation, dialogue, expunging passages, and dilating others – to her indefatigable zeal, I owe my position. All this, being independent of her participation in the performance would it not be vanity in me to add a mite of praise to that which has been showered round her throughout her life. Details were vain. No one could guess my countless obligations, had they not witnessed the conferring of them.

For the success of this play, I have to thank a most indulgent audience, an ultra-liberal management, an unrivalled cast; but little, very little is due to

The Public's
Humble Servant,
D.L.B.

*The original full version of the play was first performed on Thursday, March 4, 1841, at the Theatre Royal, Covent Garden, with the following cast:*

| | |
|---|---|
| SIR HARCOURT COURTLY | Mr W. Farren |
| MAX HARKAWAY | Mr Bartley |
| CHARLES COURTLY | Mr Anderson |
| MR SPANKER | Mr Keeley |
| DAZZLE | Mr C. Mathews |
| MARK MEDDLE | Mr Harley |
| COOL (*Valet*) | Mr Brindal |
| [1][SIMPSON] (*Butler*) | Mr Honner |
| MARTIN | Mr Ayliffe |
| [2] | |
| LADY GAY SPANKER | Mrs Nisbett |
| GRACE HARKAWAY | Madame Vestris |
| PERT | Mrs Humby |

*The Scene lies in London and Gloucestershire in 1841*
*Time – Three days*

---

[1] JAMES.
[2] *Insert:* MR SOLOMON ISAACS (presumably omitted in error).

*Ronald Eyre's adaptation was first performed on June 23, 1970, at the Aldwych Theatre, London, presented by the Royal Shakespeare Company, with the following cast:*

| | |
|---|---|
| SIR HARCOURT COURTLY | Donald Sinden |
| MAXIMILIAN HARKAWAY | Jeffery Dench |
| CHARLES COURTLY | Michael Williams |
| ADOLPHUS SPANKER | Sydney Bromley |
| DAZZLE | Barrie Ingham |
| MARK MEDDLE | Derek Smith |
| COOL, *a valet* | Anthony Pedley |
| JAMES, *a butler* | Myles Anderson |
| MARTIN | Basil Clarke |
| SOLOMON ISAACS | Leonard Fenton |
| JENKS | Christopher Biggins |
| LADY GAY SPANKER | Elizabeth Spriggs |
| GRACE HARKAWAY | Judi Dench |
| PERT | Janet Whiteside |

Directed by Ronald Eyre     Costumes by David Walker
Designed by Alan Tagg      Lighting by Stewart Leviton

ACT ONE    Scene 1: An ante-room in Sir Harcourt Courtly's house in Belgrave Square. A morning in early summer.

Scene 2: The lawn before Oak Hall, Gloucestershire. Noon the next day.

Scene 3: A drawing-room at Oak Hall. Late afternoon two days later.

ACT TWO:   Scene 1: The drawing-room. After dinner next day.

Scene 2: The lawn before Oak Hall. The following night.

Scene 3: The drawing-room. Later.

# Act One

## SCENE ONE

*An ante-room in* SIR HARCOURT COURTLY'S *house in Belgrave Square.*

*Enter* COOL.

COOL. Half-past nine, and Mr Charles has not yet returned: I am in a fever of dread. If his father happen to rise earlier than usual on any morning, he is sure to ask first for Mr Charles. Poor deluded old gentleman – he little thinks how he is deceived.

*Enter* MARTIN, *lazily.*

Well, Martin, he has not come home yet?

MARTIN. No; and I have not had a wink of sleep all night – I cannot stand this any longer; I shall give warning. This is the fifth night Mr Courtly has remained out, and I am obliged to stand at the hall window to watch for him.

COOL. You know if Sir Harcourt is aware that we connived at his son's irregularities, we should all be discharged.

MARTIN. I have used up all my common excuses on his duns. – 'Call again,' 'Not at home,' and 'Send it down to you,' won't serve any more; and Mr Crust, the wine-merchant, swears he will be paid.

COOL. So they all say. Why, he has arrests out against him already. I've seen the fellows watching the door – (*Loud knock and ring heard.*) – there he is, just in time – quick, Martin, for I expect Sir William's bell every moment – (*Bell rings.*) and there it is. (*Exit* MARTIN, *slowly.*) Thank heaven! he will return to college tomorrow, and his heavy responsibility will be taken off my shoulders. A valet is as difficult a post to fill properly as that of prime minister. (*Exit.*)

YOUNG COURTLY (*without*). Hollo!

DAZZLE (*without*). Steady!

 *Enter* YOUNG COURTLY *and* DAZZLE.

YOUNG COURTLY. Hollo-o-o!

DAZZLE. Hush! what are you about, howling like a Hottentot. Sit down there, and thank heaven you are in Belgrave Square, instead of Bow Street.

YOUNG COURTLY. D – d – damn Bow Street.

DAZZLE. Oh, with all my heart! – you have not seen as much of it as I have.

YOUNG COURTLY. I say – let me see – what was I going to say? – oh, look here – (*He pulls out a large assortment of knockers, bell-pulls, etc., from his pocket.*) There! dam'me! I'll puzzle the two-penny postmen, – I'll deprive them of their right of disturbing the neighbourhood. That black lion's head did belong to old Vampire, the money-lender; this bell-pull to Miss Stitch, the milliner.

DAZZLE. And this brass griffin –

YOUNG COURTLY. That! oh, let me see – I think – I twisted that off our own hall-door as I came in, while you were paying the cab.

DAZZLE. What shall I do with them?

YOUNG COURTLY. Pack 'em in a small hamper, and send 'em to the sitting magistrate with my father's compliments; in the meantime, come into my room and I'll astonish you with some Burgundy.

 *Re-enter* COOL.

COOL. Mr Charles –

YOUNG COURTLY. Out! out! not at home to anyone.

COOL. And drunk –

YOUNG COURTLY. As a lord.

COOL. If Sir Harcourt knew this, he would go mad, he would discharge me.

YOUNG COURTLY. You flatter yourself; that would be no proof of his insanity. – (*To* DAZZLE.) This is Cool, sir, Mr Cool; he is the best liar in London – there is a pungency about his invention, and an originality in his equivocation, that is perfectly refreshing.

COOL (*aside*). Why, Mr Charles, where did you pick him up?

YOUNG COURTLY. You mistake, he picked *me* up. (*Bell rings.*)

COOL. Here comes Sir Harcourt – pray do not let him see you in this state.

YOUNG COURTLY. State! What do you mean? I am in a beautiful state.

COOL. I should lose my character.

YOUNG COURTLY. That would be a fortunate epoch in your life, Cool.

COOL. Your father would discharge me.

YOUNG COURTLY. Cool, my dad is an old ass!

COOL. Retire to your own room, for heaven's sake, Mr Charles.

YOUNG COURTLY. I'll do so for my own sake. (*To* DAZZLE.) I say, old fellow (*Staggering*.) just hold the door steady while I go in.

DAZZLE. This way. Now, then! – take care! (*Helps him into the room.*)

 *Enter* SIR HARCOURT COURTLY *in an elegant dressing-gown and Greek skull-cap and tassels, etc.*

SIR HARCOURT. Cool, is breakfast ready?

COOL. Quite ready, Sir Harcourt.

SIR HARCOURT. Apropos. I omitted to mention that I expect Squire Harkaway to join us this morning, and you must prepare for my departure to Oak Hall immediately.

COOL. Leave town in the middle of the season, Sir Harcourt? So unprecedented a proceeding!

SIR HARCOURT. It is. I confess it, there is but one power could effect such a miracle, – that is divinity.

COOL. How!

SIR HARCOURT. In female form, of course. Cool, I am about to present society with a second Lady Courtly; young – blushing eighteen; – lovely! I have her portrait; rich! I have her banker's account; – an heiress, and a Venus!

COOL. Lady Courtly could be none other.

SIR HARCOURT. Ha! ha! Cool, your manners are above your station. – Apropos, I shall find no further use for my brocaded dressing-gown.

COOL (*bowing*). I thank you, Sir Harcourt. – Might I ask who the fortunate Lady is?

SIR HARCOURT. Certainly; Miss Grace Harkaway, the niece of my old friend, Max.

COOL. Have you never seen the lady, sir?

SIR HARCOURT. Never – that is, yes – eight years ago. Having been, as you know, on the continent for the last seven years I have not had the opportunity of paying my devoirs. Our connection and betrothal was a very extraordinary one. Her father's estates were contiguous to mine; – being a penurious miserly, *ugly* old scoundrel, he made a market of my indiscretion, and supplied my extravagance with large sums of money on mortgages, his great desire being to unite the two properties.[1] About seven years ago, he died – leaving Grace, a girl, to the guardianship of her uncle, with this[2] will: – if, on attaining the age of nineteen, she would consent to marry me, I should receive those deeds, and all his property, as her dowry. If she refused to comply with this condition, they should revert to my heir-presumptive or apparent. – She consents.

COOL. Who would not?

SIR HARCOURT. I consent to receive her £15,000 a year.

COOL (*aside*). Who would not?

SIR HARCOURT. So prepare, Cool, prepare! – But where is my boy, where is Charles?

COOL. Why – oh, he is gone out. Sir Harcourt; yes, gone out to take a walk.

SIR HARCOURT. Poor child! A perfect child in heart – a sober, placid mind – the simplicity and verdure of boyhood, kept fresh and unsullied by any contact with society. Tell me, Cool, at what time was he in bed last night?

COOL. Half-past nine, Sir Harcourt.

SIR HARCOURT. Half-past nine! Beautiful! What an original idea! Reposing in cherub slumbers, while all around him teems with drinking and debauchery! Primitive sweetness of nature! No pilot-coated, bear-skinned brawling!

COOL. Oh, Sir Harcourt!

---

[1] *Insert :* under my title.

[2] *Insert :* peculiar.

SIR HARCOURT. No cigar-smoking –

COOL. Faints at the smell of one.

SIR HARCOURT. No brandy and water bibbing –

COOL. Doesn't know the taste of anything stronger than barley-water.

SIR HARCOURT. No night parading –

COOL. Never heard the clock strike twelve, except at noon.

SIR HARCOURT. In fact, he is my son, and came a gentleman by right of paternity. He inherited my manners.

*Enter* MARTIN.

MARTIN. Mr Harkaway![1]

*Enter* MAX HARKAWAY.

MAX. Squire Harkaway, fellow, or Max Harkaway, another time. (MARTIN *bows, and exit.*) Ah! Ha! Sir Harcourt, I'm devilish glad to see ye! Gi' me your fist. Dang it, but I'm glad to see ye! Let me see. Six – seven years or more, since we have met. How quickly they have flown!

SIR HARCOURT (*throwing off his studied manner*). Max, Max! Give me your hand, old boy. – (*Aside.*) Ah! he is glad to see me. There is no fawning pretence about that squeeze. – [Cool, you may retire. (*Exit* COOL.)]

MAX. Why, you are looking quite rosy.

SIR HARCOURT. Ah! ah! Rosy! Am I too florid?

MAX. Not a bit; not a bit.

SIR HARCOURT. I thought so. – (*Aside.*) Cool said I had put too much on.

MAX. How comes it, Courtly, that you manage to retain your youth? See, I'm as grey as an old badger, or a wild rabbit; while you are – are as black as a young rook. I say, whose head grew your hair, eh?

SIR HARCOURT. Permit me to remark that all the beauties of my person are of home manufacture. Why should you be surprised at my youth? I have scarcely thrown off the giddiness of a very boy – elasticity of limb – buoyance of soul! Remark this position – (*Throws himself into an*

---

[1] *Insert :* SIR HARCOURT. Cool, you may retire.

*Exit* COOL.

*attitude*.) I held that attitude for ten minutes at Lady Acid's last *réunion*, at the express desire of one of our first sculptors, while he was making a sketch of me for the Apollo.

MAX[1] [(*aside*). Making a butt of thee for their gibes.]

SIR HARCOURT. Lady Sarah Sarcasm started up, and pointing to my face, ejaculated, 'Good gracious! Does not Sir Harcourt remind you of the countenance of Ajax, in the Pompeian portrait?'

MAX[2] [Ajax! – humbug!]

SIR HARCOURT. You are complimentary.

MAX. I'm a plain man, and always speak my mind. What's in a face or figure? Does a Grecian nose entail a good temper? Does a waspish waist indicate a good heart? Or, do oily perfumed locks necessarily thatch a well-furnished brain?

SIR HARCOURT. It's an undeniable fact, – *plain* people always praise the beauties of the *mind*.

MAX. Excuse the insinuation; I had thought the first Lady Courtly had surfeited you with beauty.

SIR HARCOURT. No; she lived fourteen months with me, and then eloped with an intimate friend. Etiquette compelled me to challenge the seducer; so I received satisfaction – and a bullet in my shoulder at the same time. However, I had the consolation of knowing that he was the handsomest man of the age. She did not insult me, by running away with a d – d ill-looking scoundrel.

MAX. That certainly was flattering.

SIR HARCOURT. I felt so, as I pocketed the ten thousand pounds damages.

MAX. That must have been a great balm to your sore honour.

SIR HARCOURT. It was – Max, my honour would have died without it; for on that year the wrong horse won the Derby – by some mistake. It was one of the luckiest chances – a thing that does not happen twice in a man's life – the opportunity of getting rid of his wife and his debts at the same time.

---

[1] I wonder you didn't do yourself an injury.
[2] A damned silly woman!

MAX. Tell the truth, Courtly! Did you not feel a little frayed in your delicacy? – your honour, now? Eh?

SIR HARCOURT. Not a whit. Why should I? I married *money* and I received it, – virgin gold! My delicacy and honour had nothing to do with hers. The world pities the bereaved husband, when it should congratulate. No, – the affair made a sensation, and I was the object. [Besides, it is vulgar to make a parade of one's feelings, however acute they may be: impenetrability of countenance is the sure sign of your highly bred man of fashion.

MAX. So, a man must, therefore, lose his wife and his money with a smile, – in fact, everything he possesses but his temper.

SIR HARCOURT. Exactly, – and greet ruin with *vive la bagatelle!* For example, – your modish beauty never discomposes the shape of her features with convulsive laughter. A smile rewards the *bon mot*, and also shows the whiteness of her teeth. She never weeps impromptu, – tears might destroy the economy of her cheek. Scenes are vulgar, – hysterics obsolete; she exhibits a calm, placid, impenetrable lake, whose surface is reflection, but of unfathomable depth, – a statue, whose life is hypothetical, and not a *prima facie* fact.

MAX. Well, give me the girl that will fly at your eyes in an argument, and stick to her point like a fox to his own tail.

SIR HARCOURT. But etiquette! Max, – remember etiquette!

MAX. Damn etiquette! I have seen a man who thought it sacrilege to eat fish with a knife, that would not scruple to rise up and rob his brother of his birthright in a gambling-house. Your thoroughbred, well-blooded heart will seldom kick over the traces of good feeling. That's my opinion, and I don't care who knows it.

SIR HARCOURT. Pardon me, – etiquette is the pulse of society, by regulating which the body politic is retained in health. I consider myself one of the faculty in the art.]

MAX. Well, well; you are a living libel upon common sense, for you are old enough to know better.

SIR HARCOURT. Old enough! What do you mean? Old! [I still retain all my little juvenile indiscretions, which your

niece's beauties must teach me to discard.] I have not sown
my wild oats yet.

MAX. Time you did, at sixty-three.

SIR HARCOURT. Sixty-three! Good God! – forty, 'pon my
life! Forty, next March.

MAX. Why, you are older than I am.

SIR HARCOURT. Oh, you are old enough to be my father!

MAX. Well, if I am, I am; that's etiquette, I suppose.[1] [Poor
Grace! How often I have pitied her fate! That a young and
beautiful creature should be driven into wretched splendour
or miserable poverty!

SIR HARCOURT. Wretched! Wherefore? Lady Courtly
wretched! Impossible!

MAX. Will she not be compelled to marry you, whether she
likes you or not? – a choice between you and poverty.
(*Aside.*) And hang me if it isn't a tie!] But why do you not
introduce your son Charles to me? I have not seen him since
he was a child. You would never permit him to accept any of
my invitations to spend his vacation at Oak Hall, – of course,
we shall have the pleasure of his company now.

SIR HARCOURT. He is not fit to enter society yet. He is a
studious, sober boy.

MAX. Boy! Why, he's five-and-twenty.

SIR HARCOURT. Good gracious! Max – you will permit me to
know my own son's age, – he is not twenty.

MAX. I'm dumb.

SIR HARCOURT. You will excuse me while I indulge in the
process of dressing. – Cool!

  *Enter* COOL.

---

[1] I must tell poor Grace about etiquette  She was expecting a
  wheezing antique for a husband. Now etiquette gives her Ajax
  and Apollo all rolled into one.

SIR HARCOURT. Well, so it does and if she's the sensible girl
  I take her for, I expect her to embrace her good fortune
  with both arms. For without me she is penniless. And so am
  I.

MAX True. Etiquette or no, that's true.

Prepare my toilet. (*Exit* COOL.) That is a ceremony, which, with me, supersedes all others. I consider it a duty which every gentleman owes to society – to render himself as agreeable an object as possible – and the least compliment a mortal can pay to nature, when she honours him by bestowing extra care in the manufacture of his person, is to display her taste to the best possible advantage; and so,[1] [*au revoir*.] (*Exit*.)

MAX. That's a good soul – he has his faults, and who has not? Forty years of age! Oh, monstrous! – But he does look uncommonly young for sixty, spite of his foreign locks and complexion.

    *Enter* DAZZLE.

DAZZLE.[2] Who's my friend, with the stick and gaiters, I wonder – one of the family – the governor maybe.

MAX. Who's this? Oh, Charles[3] [is that you, my boy? How are you? (*Aside*.) This is the *boy*.

DAZZLE. He knows me – he is too respectable for a bailiff. (*Aloud*.) How are you?

MAX. Your father has just left me.

DAZZLE (*aside*). The devil he has! He's been dead these ten years.] Oh! I see, he thinks I'm young Courtly. (*Aloud*.) The honour you would confer upon me, I must unwillingly disclaim, – I am not Mr Courtly.

MAX. I beg pardon – a friend, I suppose.

DAZZLE. Oh, a most intimate friend – a friend of years – distantly related to the family – one of my ancestors married one of his. (*Aside*.) Adam and Eve.

MAX. Are you on a visit here?

---

[1] *à bientôt.*

[2] *Insert :* (*aside, on seeing* HARKAWAY)

[3] – there you are, my boy. How are you?

DAZZLE. Beautiful. How's yourself?

MAX. Your father has just left me.

DAZZLE. Has he? He's been dead these ten years.

MAX. I expect him down on a visit.

DAZZLE (*looking up*). The devil you do.

DAZZLE. Yes. Oh! yes. (*Aside.*) Rather a short one, I'm afraid.

MAX (*aside*). This appears a dashing kind of fellow – as he is a friend of Sir Harcourt's, I'll invite him to the wedding. (*Aloud.*) Sir, if you are not otherwise engaged, I shall feel honoured by your company at my house, Oak Hall,[1] Gloucestershire.

DAZZLE. Your name is –

MAX. Harkaway – Max Harkaway.[2]

DAZZLE. Harkaway – let me see – I ought to be related to the Harkaways, somehow.

MAX. A wedding is about to come off – will you take a part on the occasion?

DAZZLE. With pleasure! Any part, but that of the husband.

MAX. Have you any previous engagement?

DAZZLE. I was thinking – eh! why, let me see. (*Aside.*) Promised to meet my tailor and his account tomorrow; however, I'll postpone that. (*Aloud.*) Have you good shooting?

MAX. Shooting! Why, there's no shooting at this time of the year.

DAZZLE.[3] [Oh! I'm in no hurry – I can wait till the season, of course.] I was only speaking precautionally – you have good shooting?

MAX. The best in the[4] [country.]

DAZZLE. Make yourself comfortable! – Say no more – I'm your man – wait till you see how I'll murder your preserves.

MAX. Do you hunt?

DAZZLE. Pardon me – but will you repeat that? (*Aside.*) Delicious and expensive idea!

MAX. You ride?

---

[1] *Insert :* Siddingham,
[2] *Insert :* DAZZLE. Richard Dazzle.
    MAX. Dazzle.
[3] Isn't there? Oh, I'm in no hurry – I can stay till the season, of course.
[4] county.

DAZZLE. Anything! Everything! From a blood to a broomstick. Only catch me a flash of lightning, and let me get on the back of it, and dam'me if I wouldn't astonish the elements.

MAX. Ha! ha!

DAZZLE. I'd put a girdle round about the earth, in very considerably less than forty minutes.

MAX. Ah! ha! We'll show old Fiddlestrings how to spend the day. [He imagines that Nature, at the earnest request of Fashion, made summer days long for him to saunter in the Park, and winter nights, that he might have good time to get cleared out at hazard or at whist.] Give me the yelping of a pack of hounds before the shuffling of a pack of cards. What state can match the chase in full cry, each vying with[1] [his fellow which shall be most happy?] A thousand deaths fly by unheeded in that one hour's life of ecstasy. Time is outrun, and Nature seems to grudge our bliss by making the day so short.

DAZZLE. No, for then rises up[2] [the idol of my great adoration.]

MAX. Who's that?

DAZZLE. The bottle – [that lends a lustre to the soul! – When the world puts on its nightcap and extinguishes the sun – then comes the bottle! Oh, mighty wine! Don't ask me to apostrophize.] Wine and love are the only two indescribable things in nature; but I prefer the wine, because its consequences [are not entailed, and] are more easily got rid of.

MAX. How so?

DAZZLE. Love ends in matrimony, wine in soda water.]

MAX. Well, I can promise you as fine a bottle as ever was cracked.

DAZZLE. Never mind the bottle, give me the wine. Say no more; but, when I arrive, just shake one of my hands, and put the key of the cellar into the other, and if I don't make myself intimately acquainted with its internal organization – well, I say nothing, – time will show.

MAX. I foresee some happy days.

---

[1] the other who can enjoy himself the most.
[2] my great idol.

DAZZLE. And I some glorious nights.

MAX. It mustn't be a flying visit.

DAZZLE. I despise the word – I'll stop a month[1] with [you].

MAX. Or a year or two.

DAZZLE. I'll live and die with you.

MAX. Ha! ha! Remember! Max Harkaway, Oak Hall,[2] Gloucestershire.

DAZZLE. I'll remember – fare ye well. (MAX *is going.*) I say, holloa! – Tallyho-o-o-o!

MAX. Yoicks! – Tallyho-o-o-o! (*Exit.*)

DAZZLE. There I am – quartered for a couple of years at the least. The old boy wants somebody to ride his horses, shoot his game, and keep a restraint on the morals of the parish: I'm eligible. What a lucky accident to meet young Courtly last night! Who could have thought it? – [3][Yesterday, I could not make certain of a dinner, except at my own proper peril; today, I would flirt with a banquet.]

*Enter* YOUNG COURTLY.

YOUNG COURTLY. What infernal row was that? Why, (*Seeing* DAZZLE.) are you here still?

DAZZLE. Yes. Ain't you delighted? I'll ring, and send the servant for my luggage.

YOUNG COURTLY. The devil you will! Why, you don't mean to say you seriously intend to take up a permanent residence here? (*He rings bell.*)

DAZZLE. Now, that's a most inhospitable insinuation.

YOUNG COURTLY. Might I ask your name?

DAZZLE. With a deal of pleasure – Richard Dazzle, late of the Unattached Volunteers, vulgarly entitled the Dirty Buffs.

*Enter* MARTIN.

YOUNG COURTLY. Then, Mr Richard Dazzle, I have the honour of wishing you a very good morning. Martin, show this gentleman the door.

---

[1] *Insert :* or two.

[2] *Insert :* Siddingham,

[3] Yesterday I could not be sure of a dinner except I stole it; today I can flirt with a banquet.

DAZZLE. If he does, I'll kick Martin out of it. – No offence. (*Exit* MARTIN.) Now, sir, permit me to place a dioramic view of your conduct before you. After bringing you safely home this morning – after indulgently waiting, whenever you took a passing fancy to a knocker or bell-pull – after conducting a retreat that would have[1] [reflected honour on] Napoleon – you would kick me into the street, like a mangy cur; and that's what you call gratitude. Now, to show you how superior I am to petty malice, I give you an unlimited invitation to my house – my country house – to remain as long as you please.

YOUNG COURTLY. Your house!

DAZZLE. Oak Hall,[2] Gloucestershire, – fine old place – for further particulars see the roadbook; that is, it *nominally* belongs to my old friend and relation, Max Harkaway; but I'm privileged. Capital old fellow – say, shall we be honoured?

YOUNG COURTLY. Sir, permit me to hesitate a moment.[3]

---

[1] done credit to

[2] *Insert :* Siddingham,

[3] *Enter* COOL.

COOL. Mr Charles – Sir Harcourt's toilet is reaching its height. He's bound to ask for you presently. Will you kindly change your trousers.

YOUNG COURTLY. Keep him at it, Cool. (*Exit* COOL.) I'm pondering. Let me see. I go back to Oxford tomorrow. So I shall not be missed here. Tradesmen begin to clamour. And there's a vixen in Curzon Street. . . . (*Enter* MARTIN.)

MARTIN. Mr Solomon Isaacs is in the hall and swears he will remain till he has arrested you.

YOUNG COURTLY. Damn me. That's awkward.

DAZZLE. Send him your compliments and lay him five to one he will not.

YOUNG COURTLY. No. (*Enter* COOL.)
Ah – Cool. Mr Isaacs lays siege to me.

COOL. I know, sir. One of many if I may say so.

YOUNG COURTLY. What would you do in my shoes, Cool?

COOL. In your shoes, sir? In your shoes I should find a friend with a castle and a moat and go into exile.

[(*Aside.*) Let me see – I go back to college tomorrow, so I shall not be missing; tradesmen begin to dun –
　*Enter* COOL.
I hear thunder; here is shelter ready for me.

COOL. Oh, Mr Charles. Mr Solomon Isaacs is in the hall, and swears he will remain till he has arrested you!

YOUNG COURTLY. Does he! – sorry he is so obstinate – take him my compliments, and I will bet him five to one he will not.

DAZZLE. Double or quits, with my kind regards.

COOL. But, sir, he has discovered the house in Curzon Street, he says he is aware the furniture, at least, belongs to you, and he will put a man in immediately.

---

SIR HARCOURT (*off*). Cool?

COOL. Coming, sir. (*To* YOUNG COURTLY.) You want my advice? Through the stables, down the mews, take a room at the Bull and wait. I'll send your things after you.

YOUNG COURTLY. God bless you, Cool. (*Exit* COOL.)

MARTIN. And Mr Isaacs, sir?

YOUNG COURTLY. Tell Mr Isaacs to go jump in the river.

DAZZLE. But quietly. (*Exit* MARTIN.)

YOUNG COURTLY. Mr Dazzle. In reply to your most generous and kind invitation, I shall feel delighted to accept it.

DAZZLE. Splendid.

SIR HARCOURT (*off*). Cool!

COOL (*off*). Have patience, sir!

MARTIN (*off*). Mr Isaacs. No, sir, please.
　YOUNG COURTLY *and* DAZZLE *exeunt fast.*
　COOL *enters and closes the door on the fleeing men.*
　MR ISAACS *enters by another door at speed.*

COOL. Good morning, Mr Isaacs.

MR ISAACS. Now see here. I take a joke. I am a humorous man. I have a little boy of my own like Mr Courtly is son to somebody. But tell him – when I see him safe in Newgate, I am happy.

COOL. Thank you, Mr Isaacs. Should I see the rash young man, I will warn him.
　*Exit* MR ISAACS *at high speed. Exit* COOL.
　　　　　CURTAIN

YOUNG COURTLY. That's awkward – what's to be done?

DAZZLE. Ask him whether he couldn't make it a woman.

YOUNG COURTLY. I must trust that to fate.

DAZZLE. I will give you my acceptance if it will be of any use to you; it is of none to me.

YOUNG COURTLY. No, sir; but in reply to your most generous and kind invitation, if you be in earnest, I shall feel delighted to accept it.

DAZZLE. Certainly.

YOUNG COURTLY. Then off we go – through the stables – down the mews, and so slip through my friend's fingers.

DAZZLE. But, stay, you must do the polite; say farewell to him before you part. Damn it, don't cut him!

YOUNG COURTLY. You jest!

DAZZLE. Here, lend me a card. (COURTLY *gives him one.*) Now, then. (*Writes.*) 'Our respects to Mr Isaacs – sorry to have been prevented from seeing him.' – Ha! ha!

YOUNG COURTLY. Ha! ha!

DAZZLE. We'll send him up some game.

YOUNG COURTLY (*to* COOL). Don't let my father see him. (*Exeunt.*)

COOL. What's this? – 'Mr Charles Courtly, P.P.C., returns thanks for obliging inquiries.' (*Exit.*)]

# Act Two[1]

## SCENE ONE

*The lawn before Oak Hall, a fine Elizabethan Mansion; a drawing-room is seen through large French windows at the back. Statues, urns, and garden chairs about the stage.*

*Enter* PERT[2] [*and* JAMES.]

[3][PERT. James. Miss Grace desires me to request that you will watch at the avenue, and let her know when the squire's carriage is seen on the London road.

JAMES. I will go to the lodge. (*Exit.*)]

PERT. How I do long to see what kind of a man Sir Harcourt Courtly is! They say he is sixty; so he must be old, and consequently ugly. If I was Miss Grace, I would rather give up all my fortune and marry the man I liked, than go to church with a stuffed eel-skin. But taste is everything, – she doesn't seem to care whether he is sixty or sixteen; jokes at love; prepares for matrimony as she would for dinner; [says it is a necessary evil, and what can't be cured must be endured.] Now, I say this is against all nature; and she is either no woman, or a deeper one than I am, if she prefers an old man to a young one.[4] [Here she comes! looking as cheer-

---

[1] ACT ONE, SCENE TWO.

[2] JAMES *is decorating a wheelbarrow with flowers.*

[3] PERT. James, I thought Miss Grace desired you to watch at the lodge for the squire's carriage to happen on the London road.

JAMES. You thought aright. And Miss Grace gave me further permission to decorate aforehand.

*Exit* JAMES *with wheelbarrow.*

[4] I prefer Mr Jenks, my Mr Jenks. Oh, Jenks. When will you say the nuptial word?

fully as if she was going to marry Mr Jenks! my Mr Jenks! who nobody won't lead to the halter till I have that honour.]

*Enter* GRACE *from the drawing-room.*

GRACE. Well, Pert? any sign of the squire yet?

PERT. No, Miss Grace; but James has gone to watch the road.

GRACE. In my uncle's letter he mentions a Mr Dazzle, whom he has invited; so you must[1] prepare a room for him. He is some friend of my husband that is to be, and my uncle seems to have taken an extraordinary predilection for him. Apropos! I must not forget to have a[2] [bouquet] for the dear old man when he arrives.

[3][PERT. The dear old man! Do you mean Sir Harcourt?

GRACE. Law! no, my uncle, of course. (*Plucking flowers.*) What do I care for Sir Harcourt Courtly?]

PERT. Isn't it odd, Miss, you have never seen your intended, [though it has been so long since you were betrothed?][4]

GRACE. Not at all; marriage matters are conducted nowadays in a most mercantile manner; consequently a previous acquaintance is by no means indispensable. Besides, my *prescribed* husband has been upon the continent for the benefit of his – property! They say a southern clime is a great restorer of consumptive estates.

PERT. [5][Well, Miss, for my own part, I should like to have a good look at my bargain before I paid for it; 'specially when one's life is the price of the article.] But why, ma'am, do you consent to marry in this blind-man's-buff sort of manner? What would you think if he were not quite so old?

GRACE. I should think he was a little younger.

---

[1] *Insert:* tell Mrs Howton to
[2] flower
[3] PERT. The dear old man! Oh madam, how could you?
GRACE. My uncle is the dear old man – whereas Sir Harcourt Courtly has yet to prove himself.
[4] though you've been so long betrothed?
[5] Well, Miss, for my own part, I like to look at my article before I buy it. It's the only way to be sure of a bargain.

PERT. Well, I should like him all the better.[1]

GRACE. That wouldn't I. A young husband might expect affection and nonsense, which 'twould be deceit in me to render; nor would he permit me to remain with my uncle. – Sir Harcourt takes me with the incumbrances on his estate, and I shall beg to be left among the rest of the livestock.

PERT. Ah, Miss! but some day you might chance to stumble over *the* man, – what could you do then?

GRACE. Do! beg *the* man's pardon, and request *the* man to pick me up again.

PERT. Ah! you were never in love, Miss?

GRACE. I never was, nor will be, till I am tired of myself and common sense. Love is a pleasant scape-goat for a little epidemic madness. I must have been inoculated in my infancy, for the infection passes over poor me in contempt.
    *Enter* JAMES.

JAMES. Two gentlemen, Miss Grace, have just alighted.

GRACE. Very well, James. (*Exit* JAMES.) [2][Love is pictured as a boy; in another century they will be wiser, and paint him as a fool, with a cap and bells, without a thought above the jingling of his own folly. Now, Pert, remember this as a maxim, – A woman is always in love with one of two things.

PERT. What are they, Miss?

GRACE. A man, or herself – and I know which is the most profitable. (*Exit.*)

PERT. I wonder what my Jenks would say, if I was to ask him. Law! here comes Mr Meddle, his rival, contemporary

---

[1]*Insert :* young.

[2] PERT. Do you feel nothing stirring, Miss?

GRACE. I feel the wind on my cheek, the stinging nettle at my ankle and the scent of flowers round my nose. What more should I feel?
    *Exit* GRACE.

PERT. That's books for you. Oh Jenks, take care. There's books on your dear little shelves as well. (*Cows low.*)
    Law! Here comes Mr Meddle, his rival at law and deadliest enemy. At the gallop too. Now what brings him here?
    *She retires.*

solicitor, as he calls him, – a nasty, prying, ugly wretch – what brings him here? He comes puffed with some news. (*Retires.*)]

   *Enter* MEDDLE, *with a newspaper.*

MEDDLE. I have secured the only newspaper in the village[1] my character as an attorney-at-law depended on the monopoly of its information. – I took it up by chance when this paragraph met my astonished view: (*Reads.*) 'We understand that the contract of marriage so long in abeyance on account of the lady's minority, is about to be celebrated, at Oak Hall, Gloucestershire, the well-known and magnificent mansion of Maxmilian Harkaway, Esq., between Sir Harcourt Courtly, Baronet, of fashionable celebrity, and Miss Grace Harkaway, niece to the said Mr Harkaway. The preparations are proceeding on the good old English style.' Is it possible! I seldom swear, except in a witness box, but damme, had it been known in the village, my reputation would have been lost; my voice in the parlour of the Red Lion mute, and Jenks, a fellow who calls himself a lawyer, without more capability than a broomstick, and as much impudence as a young barrister, after getting a verdict, by mistake; why, he would actually have taken the Reverend Mr Spout by the button,[2] which is now my sole privilege. Ah! here is Mrs Pert; [couldn't have hit upon a better person.] I'll cross-examine her – [Lady's maid to Miss Grace, confidential purloiner of second-hand silk – a *nisi prius* of her mistress – Ah! sits on the woolsack in the pantry, and dictates the laws of kitchen etiquette. –] Ah! Mrs Pert, good morning; permit me to say, – and my word as a legal character is not unduly considered – I venture to affirm, that you look a – quite like the – a –[3]

---

[1] *Insert :* before Jenks got his thieving hands on it.
[2] *Insert :* and got himself the drawing up of the contract
[3] Have you read the paper, madam?

PERT. No.

MEDDLE. Floods in Norfolk. Her Majesty gone mad again and vulgar disorders at Lambeth Palace.

[PERT. Law! Mr Meddle.

MEDDLE. Exactly like the Law.

PERT. Ha! indeed; complimentary, I confess; like the law; tedious, prosy, made up of musty paper. You shan't have a long suit of me. Good morning! (*Going.*)

MEDDLE. Stay, Mrs Pert; don't calumniate my calling, or disseminate vulgar prejudices.]

PERT. Vulgar! you talk of vulgarity to me! you, [1][whose sole employment is to sneak] about like a pig, snouting out the dust-hole of society, and feeding upon the bad ends of vice! you, [who live upon the world's iniquity;] you miserable specimen of a bad six-and-eightpence!

MEDDLE. But, Mrs Pert –

PERT. Don't but me, sir; I won't be butted by any such[2] [low fellow.]

MEDDLE. This is slander; an action will lie.

[3][PERT. Let it lie; lying is your trade. I'll tell you what, Mr Meddle; If I had my will, I would soon put a check on your prying propensities. I'd treat you as the farmers do the inquisitive hogs.

MEDDLE. How?

PERT. I would ring your nose.] (*Exit.*)

MEDDLE. Not much information elicited from that witness. Jenks is at the bottom of this. I have very little hesitation in saying, Jenks is a libellous rascal; I heard reports that he was undermining my character here, through Mrs Pert. Now I'm certain of it. Assault is expensive; but I certainly will put by a small weekly stipendium, until I can afford to kick Jenks.

DAZZLE (*outside*). Come along; this way!

MEDDLE. Ah! whom have we here? Visitors; I'll address them.

---

[1] who sneak

[2] old ram.

[3] PERT (*seizing and tearing up his paper and notepad*). And this is theft. And this is violation of property. And this is defacing a gentleman's garden. And this is the spreading of good news. If you take my advice, Mr Meddle, you'll collect up your snivelling litter and shift to another sty.

*Enter* DAZZLE.[1]

DAZZLE. Who's this, I wonder; one of the family? I must know him. (*To* MEDDLE.) Ah! how are ye?

MEDDLE. Quite well. Just arrived? – ah! – um! – Might I request the honour of knowing whom I address?

DAZZLE. Richard Dazzle, Esquire; and you –

MEDDLE. Mark Meddle, Attorney-at-law.

[2]

*Enter* YOUNG COURTLY.

DAZZLE. What detained you?

YOUNG COURTLY. My dear fellow, I have just seen such a woman!

DAZZLE (*aside*).[3] [Hush!] (*Aloud.*) Permit me to introduce you to my very old friend, Meddle. He's a capital fellow; know him.

MEDDLE. I feel honoured. Who is your friend?

DAZZLE, Oh, he? What, my friend? Oh! Augustus Hamilton.

YOUNG COURTLY. How d'ye do? (*Looking off.*) There she is again!

[4][MEDDLE (*looking off*). Why, that is Miss Grace.

DAZZLE. Of course, Grace.]

YOUNG COURTLY. I'll go and introduce myself.

DAZZLE *stops him.*

DAZZLE (*aside*). What are you about? would you insult my old friend, Puddle, by running away? (*Aloud.*) I say, Puddle, just show my friend the lions, while I say how d'ye do to

---

[1] *Insert: preceded by* JAMES *and his wheelbarrow loaded with luggage.* JAMES *crosses the stage.*

[2] *Insert:*

DAZZLE. Not *the* Mark Meddle?

MEDDLE. Well, sir, I wouldn't swear to a monopoly of the name but the only Mark Meddle hereabouts and not counting Jenks the only attorney –

*During this,* JAMES *re-crosses the stage and exits.*

[3] *Manners!*

[4] MEDDLE (*looking off*). Ah, the divine Miss Grace.

DAZZLE. Of course, the divine Grace.

my young friend, Grace. (*Aside.*) Cultivate his acquaintance.

(*Exit* – YOUNG COURTLY *looks after him.*)

MEDDLE. [1][Mr Hamilton, might I take the liberty?]

YOUNG COURTLY (*looking off*). Confound the fellow!

MEDDLE. Sir, what did you remark?

YOUNG COURTLY. She's gone! Oh, are you here still, Mr Thingomerry Puddle?

MEDDLE. Meddle, sir, Meddle, in the list of attorneys.

YOUNG COURTLY. Well, Muddle, or Puddle, or whoever you are, you are a bore.

MEDDLE (*aside*). How excessively odd! Mrs Pert said I was a pig; now I'm a boar! I wonder what they'll make of me next.[2]

YOUNG COURTLY. Mr Thingamy, will you take a word of advice?

MEDDLE. Feel honoured.

YOUNG COURTLY. Get out.

MEDDLE. Do you mean to – I don't understand.

YOUNG COURTLY. Delighted to quicken your apprehension. You are an ass, Puddle.

MEDDLE, Ha! ha! another quadruped! Yes; beautiful – (*Aside.*) I wish he'd call me something libellous; but that would be too much to expect – (*Aloud.*) Anything else?

YOUNG COURTLY. Some miserable, pettifogging scoundrel!

MEDDLE. Good! ha! ha!

YOUNG COURTLY. What do you mean by laughing at me?

MEDDLE. Ha! ha! ha! excellent! delicious!

YOUNG COURTLY. Mr – [3] – are you ambitious of a kicking?

MEDDLE. Very, very – Go on – kick – go on.

YOUNG COURTLY (*looking off*). Here she comes! I'll speak to her.

---

[1] Oak Hall, sir, earns a place in the Doomsday Book, though little of that ancient structure remains except a wall of the pigsty, which is of Saxon origin.

[2] *Insert*: The Roman invader left his corn supplies under the shelter of these oaks –.

[3] *Insert*: MEDDLE. Meddle.

MEDDLE. But, sir – sir –

YOUNG COURTLY. Oh, go to the devil! (*He runs off.*)

MEDDLE. There's a chance lost – gone! I have no hesitation in saying that, in another minute, I should have been kicked; literally kicked – a legal luxury. Costs, damages, and actions rose up like sky-rockets in my aspiring soul. With golden tails reaching to the infinity of my hopes, (*Looking.*) – they are coming this way, Mr Hamilton in close conversation with Lady Courtly that is to be. Crim. Con. – Courtly versus Hamilton – damages problematical – Meddle, chief witness for plaintiff; guinea a day – professional man! I'll take down their conversation verbatim. (*He retires behind a bush.*)

*Enter* GRACE, *followed by* YOUNG COURTLY.

GRACE. Perhaps you would follow your friend into the dining-room; refreshment after your long journey must be requisite.

YOUNG COURTLY. Pardon me, madam; but the lovely garden and the loveliness before me is better refreshment than I could procure in any dining-room.

GRACE. Ha! Your company and compliments arrive together.

YOUNG COURTLY. I trust that a passing remark will not spoil so welcome an introduction as this by offending you.

GRACE. I am not certain that anything you could say would offend me.

YOUNG COURTLY. I never meant –

GRACE. I thought not. In turn, pardon me, when I request you will commence your visit with this piece of information: I consider compliments impertinent, and sweetmeat language fulsome.

YOUNG COURTLY. I would condemn my tongue to a Pythagorean silence if I thought it could attempt to flatter.

GRACE. It strikes me, sir, that you are a stray bee from the hive of fashion; if so, reserve your honey for its proper cell. [A truce to compliments] – You have just arrived *from town*, I apprehend.

YOUNG COURTLY. This moment I left mighty London, under the fever of a full season, groaning with the noisy pulse of wealth and the giddy whirl of fashion. Enchanting, busy London! how have I prevailed on myself to desert you! Next week the new ballet comes out, – the week after comes Ascot. – Oh!

GRACE. [1][How agonizing must be the reflection.]

YOUNG COURTLY. Torture! Can you inform me how you manage to avoid suicide here? If there was but an opera even within twenty miles! We couldn't get up a rustic ballet among the village girls? No? – ah!

GRACE. I am afraid you would find that difficult. How I contrive to support life I don't know – it is wonderful – but I have not precisely contemplated suicide yet, nor do I miss the opera.

YOUNG COURTLY. How can you manage to kill time?

GRACE. I can't. Men talk of killing time, while time quietly kills them. I have many employments – this week I devote to study and various amusements – next week to being married – the following week to repentance, perhaps.

YOUNG COURTLY. Married!

GRACE. You seem surprised; I believe it is of frequent occurrence in the metropolis. – Is it not?

YOUNG COURTLY. Might I ask to whom?

GRACE. A gentleman who has been strongly recommended to me for the situation of husband.

[2][YOUNG COURTLY. What an extraordinary match! Would you not consider it advisable to see him, previous to incurring the consequences of such an act?

GRACE. You must be aware that fashion says otherwise. The gentleman swears eternal devotion to the lady's fortune, and the lady swears she will outvie him still. My Lord's horses, and my lady's diamonds, shine through a few seasons, until a seat in Parliament, or the continent, stares them in the face;

---

[1] It must hurt to think about it.
[2] YOUNG COURTLY. Recommended? Would you not consider it advisable to see him first?
GRACE. See him? No, sir. I might be led to dispute the conditions of the sale.

then, when thrown upon each other for resources of comfort, they begin to quarrel about the original conditions of the sale.]

YOUNG COURTLY. Sale! No! that would be degrading civilization into a Turkish barbarity.

GRACE. Worse, sir, a great deal worse; [1][for there at least they do not attempt concealment of the barter]; but here, every London ball-room is a marriage mart – young ladies are trotted out, while the mother, father, or chaperone plays auctioneer, and knocks them down to the highest bidder, – young men are ticketed up with their fortunes on their backs, – and Love, turned into a dapper showman, descants on the excellent qualities of the material.

[2][YOUNG COURTLY. Oh! that such a custom could have ever emanated from the healthy soil of an English heart!

GRACE. No. It never did – like most of our literary dandyisms and dandy literature, it was borrowed from the French.

YOUNG COURTLY. You seem to laugh at love.

GRACE. Love! why, the very word is a breathing satire upon a man's reason – a mania, indigenous to humanity – nature's jester, who plays off tricks upon the world, and trips up common sense. When I'm in love, I'll write an almanac, for very lack of wit – prognosticate the sighing season – when to beware of tears – about this time, expect matrimony to be prevalent! Ha! ha! Why should I lay out my life in love's bonds upon the bare security of a man's word?]

---

[1] For the Turks at least do not attempt concealment of the barter.

[2] YOUNG COURTLY. Oh! That such a custom could have ever sprung from the healthy soil of England.

GRACE. It didn't. It was borrowed from the French.

YOUNG COURTLY. You seem to laugh at love.

GRACE. Love! why the very word is a breathing satire upon a man's reason. When I'm in love, I'll write a penny almanac for lovesick ladies – how to prognosticate the sighing season – when to beware of tears – about this time expect matrimony to be prevalent! Why should I hazard my life upon the bare security of a man's word?

[1][*Enter* JAMES.

JAMES. The squire, madam, has just arrived, and another gentleman with him.

GRACE (*aside*). My intended, I suppose. (*Exit* JAMES.)]

YOUNG COURTLY. I perceive you are one of the railers against what is termed the follies of high life.

GRACE. [2][No, not particularly; I deprecate all folly. By what prerogative can the west-end mint issue absurdity, which, if coined in the east, would be voted vulgar?]

YOUNG COURTLY. By a sovereign right – because it has Fashion's head upon its side, and that stamps it current.

[3][GRACE. Poor Fashion, for how many sins has thou to answer! The gambler pawns his birth-right for fashion – the *roué* steals his friend's wife for fashion – each abandons himself to the storm of impulse, calling it the breeze of fashion.

YOUNG COURTLY. Is this idol of the world so radically vicious?

GRACE. No; the root is well enough, as the body was, until it had outgrown its native soil; but now], like a mighty giant lying over Europe, it pillows its head in Italy, its heart in France, leaving the heels alone its sole support for England.

[YOUNG COURTLY. Pardon me, madam, you wrong yourself to rail against your own inheritance – the kingdom to which loveliness and wit attest your title.

GRACE. A mighty realm, forsooth, – with milliners for ministers, a cabinet of coxcombs, envy for my homage, ruin for my revenue – my right of rule depending on the shape of a bonnet or the sit of a pelisse, with the next grand noddle as my heir-apparent. Mr Hamilton, when I am crowned, I shall feel happy to abdicate in your favour.] (*Curtseys and exit.*)

---

[1] *Enter* PERT.

PERT. They're here, madam. Oh, madam, they're here.

GRACE. Thank you, Pert. (*Exit* PERT.)

[2] No, not high life particularly; I deplore all folly. By what prerogative can the West End mint issue absurdity, which, if coined in the East, would be reckoned vulgar?

[3] GRACE. Poor fashion! It has outgrown its native soil and now

YOUNG COURTLY. [1][What did she mean by that?] Hang me if I can understand her – she is evidently not used to society. Ha! – [takes every word I say for infallible truth] – requires the solution of a compliment, as if it were a problem in Euclid. She said she was about to marry, but I rather imagine she was in jest. [2]['Pon my life, I feel very queer at the contemplation of such an idea – I'll follow her.] (MEDDLE *comes down.*) Oh! perhaps this booby can inform me something about her. (MEDDLE *makes signs at him.*) What the devil is he at!

MEDDLE. It won't do – no – ah! um – it's not to be done.

YOUNG COURTLY. What do you mean?

MEDDLE (*points after* GRACE). Counsel retained – cause to come off!

YOUNG COURTLY. Cause to come off!

MEDDLE. Miss Grace is about to be married.

YOUNG COURTLY. Is it possible?

MEDDLE. Certainly. If *I* have the drawing out of the deeds –

YOUNG COURTLY. To whom?

MEDDLE. Ha! hem! Oh, yes! I dare say – Information being scarce in the market, I hope to make mine valuable.

YOUNG COURTLY. Married! married!

MEDDLE. Now I shall have another chance.

YOUNG COURTLY. I'll run and ascertain the truth of this from Dazzle. (*Exit.*)

MEDDLE. It's of no use: he either dare not kick me, or he can't afford it – in either case, he is beneath my notice. Ah! who comes here? – can it be Sir Harcourt Courtly himself? It can be no other. (*Enter* COOL.[3]) Sir, I have the honour to bid you welcome to Oak Hall and the village of [Oldborough.][4]

COOL (*aside.*) Excessively polite. (*Aloud.*) – Sir, thank you.

MEDDLE. The township contains two thousand inhabitants.

---

[1] What an enchanting little devil!
[2] 'Pon my life, I feel very queer at the contemplation of it.
[3] *Insert: preceded by* JAMES *with loaded barrow.*
[4] Siddingham.

COOL. Does it! I am delighted to hear it.

MEDDLE (*aside*). I can charge him for that – ahem – six and eightpence is not much – but it is a beginning. (*Aloud.*) If you will permit me, I can inform you of the different commodities for which it is famous.

COOL. Much obliged – but here comes Sir Harcourt Courtly, my master and Mr Harkaway – any other time I shall feel delighted.

MEDDLE. Oh! (*Aside.*) Mistook the man for the master. [1][(*He retires up.*)

*Enter* MAX *and* SIR HARCOURT.

MAX. Here we are at last. Now give ye welcome to Oak Hall, Sir Harcourt, heartily!]

SIR HARCOURT (*languidly*). Cool, assist me.

COOL *takes off his furred cloak and gloves; gives him white gloves and a white handkerchief.*

MAX. [Why, you require unpacking as carefully as my best bin of port.] Well, [now you are decanted,] tell me, what did you think of my park as we came along?

SIR HARCOURT. That it would never come to an end. You said it was only a stone's throw from your infernal lodge to the house; why, it's ten miles at least.[2]

MAX. I'll do it in ten minutes any day.

SIR HARCOURT. Yes, in a steam carriage. Cool, perfume my handkerchief.

MAX. Don't do it. Don't! perfume in the country![3] [why, it's high treason in the very face of Nature]; 'tis introducing the robbed to the robber. Here are the sweets from which your fulsome essences are pilfered, and libelled with their names, – don't insult them, too.

SIR HARCOURT (*to* MEDDLE). Oh! cull me a bouquet, my man!

---

[1] PERT *and* JAMES *run in and line up.* MEDDLE *joins them.*

MAX. Here we are at last. Now give ye welcome to Oak Hall, Sir Harcourt, heartily! Fetch Miss Grace, Pert.

SIR HARCOURT. A moment, Max, for pity's sake.

[2] *Insert :* – and all of it upward.

[3] why, it's a slap in the very face of Nature.

MAX (*turning*). Ah, Meddle! how are you? This is Lawyer Meddle.

SIR HARCOURT. Oh! I took him for one of your people.

MEDDLE. Ah[1]! [naturally] – um – Sir Harcourt Courtly, I have the honour to congratulate – happy occasion approaches. Ahem! I have no hesitation in saying this *very* happy occasion approaches.

[2][SIR HARCOURT. Cool, is the conversation addressed towards me?

COOL. I believe so, Sir Harcourt.

MEDDLE. Oh, certainly! I was complimenting you.

SIR HARCOURT. Sir, you are very good; the honour is undeserved; but I am only in the habit of receiving compliments from the fair sex. Men's admiration is so damnably insipid.

MEDDLE. I had hoped to make a unit on that occasion.

SIR HARCOURT. Yes, and you hoped to put an infernal number of ciphers after your unit on that and any other occasion.]

MEDDLE. Ha! ha! very good. Why, I did hope to have the honour of drawing out the deeds;[3] for, whatever Jenks may say to the contrary, I have no hesitation in saying –

SIR HARCOURT (*putting him aside; to* MAX). If the future Lady Courtly be visible at so unfashionable an hour as this, I shall beg to be introduced.

[4][MAX. Visible! Ever since six this morning, I'll warrant ye. Two to one she is at dinner.

---

[1] understandably

[2] SIR HARCOURT. Cool, is this rhapsody addressed towards me?
COOL. I believe so, Sir Harcourt.
MEDDLE. The law presents its compliments.
SIR HARCOURT. Very civil of it.

[3] *Insert:* on that occasion

[4] MAX. Visible! Up since six this morning, I'll warrant ye. Two to one she is busy with dinner.
SIR HARCOURT. Dinner! Is it possible anyone should dine at half-past one p.m.?
MEDDLE. I rather prefer that hour to peck a little morsel –

SIR HARCOURT. Dinner! Is it possible? Lady Courtly dine at half-past one P.M.!

MEDDLE. I rather prefer that hour to peck a little my –]

SIR HARCOURT. Dear me! who was addressing you?

MEDDLE. Oh! I beg pardon.

MAX. [1][Here, James! (*Calling; enter* JAMES.) Tell Miss Grace to come here directly. (*Exit* JAMES.)] Now prepare, Courtly, for, though I say it, she *is* – with the exception of my bay mare, Kitty – the handsomest thing in the [2][country]. Considering she is a biped, she is a wonder! Full of blood, sound wind and limb, plenty of bone, sweet coat, in fine condition, with a thoroughbred step, [as dainty as a pet greyhound.]

SIR HARCOURT. Damme, don't compare her to a horse!

MAX. Well, I wouldn't, but she's almost as fine a creature, – close similarities.

MEDDLE. Oh, very fine creature! Close similarity amounting to identity.

SIR HARCOURT. Good gracious, sir! What can a lawyer know about women!

[3][MEDDLE. Everything. The consistorial court is a fine study of the character, and I have no hesitation in saying that I have examined more women than Jenks, or –]

SIR HARCOURT. Oh, damn Jenks!

MEDDLE. Sir, thank you. Damn him again, sir, damn him again!

    *Enter* GRACE.

GRACE. My dear uncle!

---

[1] Pert, tell Miss Grace to come here directly.
    *Exit* PERT.

[2] county.

[3] MEDDLE. Everything. The consistorial court is a fine study of the character –
SIR HARCOURT. Am I the thing, Cool?
COOL. Quite the thing, sir.
MEDDLE. – And I have no hesitation in saying that I have examined more women than Jenks, or –

MAX. Ah, Grace, you little jade, come here.

SIR HARCOURT (*eyeing her through his glass*). Oh, dear! she is a rural Venus! I'm astonished and delighted.

MAX. Won't you kiss your old uncle? (*He kisses her.*)

SIR HARCOURT (*draws an agonizing face*). Oh! – ah – um! – [*N'importe!*] – my privilege in embryo – [hem! It's very tantalizing, though.]

MAX. You are not glad to see me, you are not. (*Kissing her.*)

SIR HARCOURT. Oh; no, no! (*Aside.*) That is too much. I shall do something horrible presently, [if this goes on.] (*Aloud.*) I should be sorry to curtail any little ebullition of affection; but – ahem! May I be permitted?

MAX. Of course you may. There, Grace, is Sir Harcourt, your husband that will be. Go to him, girl.

SIR HARCOURT. Permit me to do homage to the charms, the presence of which have placed me in sight of Paradise.

   SIR HARCOURT *and* GRACE *retire. Enter* DAZZLE.

DAZZLE. Ah! old fellow, how are you?

MAX. I'm glad to see you! Are you comfortably quartered, yet, eh?

DAZZLE. Splendidly quartered! What a place you've got here! Here, Hamilton. (*Enter* YOUNG COURTLY.) Permit me to introduce my friend, Augustus Hamilton. (*Aside.*) Capital fellow! drinks like a sieve, and rides like a thunderstorm.

MAX. Sir, I'm devilish glad to see you. Here, Sir Harcourt, permit me to introduce to you –

YOUNG COURTLY. The devil!

DAZZLE (*aside*). What's the matter?

YOUNG COURTLY (*aside*). Why, that is my governor, by Jupiter!

DAZZLE (*aside*). What, old Whiskers? [1][you don't say that!]

YOUNG COURTLY (*aside*). It is; what's to be done now?

MAX. Mr Hamilton, Sir Harcourt Courtly – [Sir Harcourt Courtly,] Mr Hamilton.

---

[1] you don't say so!

SIR HARCOURT. [1] Hamilton! Good gracious! God bless me! – why, Charles, is it possible? – why, Max, that's my son!

[YOUNG COURTLY (*aside*). What shall I do!]

MAX. Your son!

GRACE. Your son, Sir Harcourt! have you a son as old as that gentleman!

SIR HARCOURT. No – that is – a – yes, – not by twenty years – a – Charles, why don't you answer me, sir?

YOUNG COURTLY (*aside to* DAZZLE). What shall I say?

DAZZLE (*aside*). Deny your identity.

YOUNG COURTLY (*aside*). Capital! (*Aloud.*) [2][What's the matter, sir?]

SIR HARCOURT. How came you down here, sir?

YOUNG COURTLY. By one of Newman's – best fours – in twelve hours and a quarter.

SIR HARCOURT. Isn't your name Charles Courtly?

YOUNG COURTLY. Not to my knowledge.

SIR HARCOURT. Do you mean to say that you are usually called Augustus Hamilton?

YOUNG COURTLY. Lamentable fact – and quite correct.

SIR HARCOURT. Cool, is that my son?

COOL. No, sir – it is not Mr Charles – but is very like him.

MAX. I cannot understand all this.

GRACE (*aside*). I think I can.

DAZZLE (*aside to* YOUNG COURTLY). Give him a touch of the indignant.

[YOUNG COURTLY. [3]Allow me to say, Sir What-d'ye-call-'em Hartly –]

SIR HARCOURT. Hartly, sir! Courtly, sir! Courtly!

YOUNG COURTLY. Well, Hartly, or [4][Courtheart] or whatever your name may be, I say your conduct is – a – a –, and were it

---

[1] *Insert :* How do you do? (SIR HARCOURT *turns back to* GRACE ; *then turns suddenly to* YOUNG COURTLY.)

[2] What's the matter with you, sir?

[3] Allow me to say, Sir What-d'ye-call 'em Carthorse Hartly.

DAZZLE. Sir, Workhouse Partly.

[4] Cartly

not the for the presence of this lady, I should feel inclined –
to – to – [1]

SIR HARCOURT. No, no, that can't be my son, – he never
would address me in that way.[2]

MAX. What is all this?

SIR HARCOURT. Sir, your likeness to my son Charles is so
astonishing, that it, for a moment – the equilibrium of my
etiquette – 'pon my life, I – permit me to request your
pardon.

MEDDLE (*to* SIR HARCOURT). Sir Harcourt, don't apologize,
don't – bring an action. I'm witness.

SIR HARCOURT. Someone take this man away.

[*Enter* JAMES.[3]

JAMES. Luncheon is on the table, sir.]

SIR HARCOURT. Miss Harkaway, I never swore before a lady
in my life – except when I promised to love and cherish the
late Lady Courtly, which I took care to preface with an
apology, – I was compelled to the ceremony, and consequently not answerable for the language – but [4][to
that gentleman's identity I would have pledged – my
hair.

GRACE (*aside*). If that security were called for, I suspect the
answer would be – no effects.] (*Exeunt* SIR HARCOURT *and*
GRACE.)

MEDDLE (*to* MAX). I have something very particular to com-
municate.

MAX. Can't listen at present. (*Exit*.)

---

[1] *Insert:* DAZZLE. Go it. Say you would kick him –

YOUNG COURTLY. To punish your impertinence with a sound
    kicking.

MEDDLE. Kicking! Kicking!

[2] *Insert:* MEDDLE. My dear madam, withdraw to oblige me. He
    will kick somebody after all.

[3] *A Gong sounds.*

GRACE. Luncheon is on the table. Will you come, sir?

[4] I swear, if he were a year or two younger, that is my son.

GRACE. A year or two makes all the difference.

MEDDLE (*to* DAZZLE *and* YOUNG COURTLY). I can afford you information which I –

DAZZLE. Oh, don't bother!

YOUNG COURTLY. Go to the devil! (*Exeunt.*)

MEDDLE. Now, I have no hesitation in saying that is the height of ingratitude. – Oh – Mr Cool – can you oblige me? (*Presents his account.*)

COOL. Why, what is all this?

MEDDLE. Small account *versus* you – to giving information concerning the last census of the population of [1][Oldborough] and vicinity, six and eightpence.

COOL. Oh, you mean to make me pay for this, do you?

MEDDLE. Unconditionally.

COOL. Well, I have no objection – the charge is fair – but remember, I am a servant on board wages, – will you throw in a little advice gratis – if I give you the money?

MEDDLE. Ahem! – I will.

COOL. A fellow has insulted me. I want to abuse him – what terms are actionable?

MEDDLE. You may call him anything you please, providing there are no witnesses.

COOL. Oh, may I? (*Looks round.*) [2][– then you rascally, pettifogging scoundrel!]

MEDDLE. Hallo!

COOL. You mean – dirty – disgrace to your profession.

MEDDLE. Libel – slander –

COOL. Aye, but where are your witnesses?

MEDDLE. Give me the costs – six and eightpence.

COOL. I deny that you gave me information at all.

MEDDLE. You do!

COOL. Yes, where are your witnesses? (*Exit.*)

MEDDLE. Ah – damme![3] (*Exit.*)

---

[1] Siddingham

[2] then you, Meddle, are a rascally pettifogging scoundrel!

[3] *Insert :* (*Shouts.*) Londoner!

# [1]Act Three

## *SCENE ONE*

*A morning-room in Oak Hall, French windows opening to the lawn.*

MAX *and* SIR HARCOURT *seated together on one side,* DAZZLE *on the other;* GRACE *and* YOUNG COURTLY *are playing chess at back. All dressed for dinner.*

MAX (*aside to* SIR HARCOURT). What can I do?

SIR HARCOURT. Get rid of them civilly.

MAX. What, turn them out, after I particularly invited them to stay a month or two?

SIR HARCOURT. Why, they are disreputable characters; as for that young fellow, in whom my Lady Courtly appears so particularly absorbed, – I am bewildered – [2][I have written to town for my Charles, my boy] – it certainly is the most extraordinary likeness –

DAZZLE. Sir Harcourt, I have an idea –

SIR HARCOURT. Sir, I am delighted to hear it. – (*Aside.*) That fellow is a swindler.

MAX. I met him at your house.

SIR HARCOURT. Never saw him before in all my life.

DAZZLE (*crossing to* SIR HARCOURT). I will bet you five to one that I can beat you three out of four games at billiards, with one hand.

SIR HARCOURT. No, sir.

DAZZLE. I don't mind giving you ten points in fifty.

SIR HARCOURT. Sir, I never gamble.

---

[1] ACT ONE, SCENE THREE.

[2] I have sent for my boy Charles to come and face it out with him.

DAZZLE. You don't! Well, I'll teach you – easiest thing in life – you have every requisite – good temper.

SIR HARCOURT. I have not, sir.

DAZZLE. A long-headed, knowing old buck.

SIR HARCOURT. Sir!

[1][*They go up conversing with* MAX.]

GRACE. Really, Mr Hamilton, you improve. – A young man pays us a visit, as you half intimate, to escape inconvenient friends – that is complimentary to us, his hosts.

YOUNG COURTLY. Nay, that is too severe.

GRACE. After an acquaintanceship of two days, you sit down to teach me chess, and domestic economy at the same time. – Might I ask where you graduated in that science – where you learned all that store of matrimonial advice which you have obliged me with?

YOUNG COURTLY. I [2][inhibited] it, madam, from the moment I beheld you, and having studied my subject *con amore*, took my degrees from your eyes.[3]

GRACE. Oh, I see you are a Master of Arts already.

YOUNG COURTLY. Unfortunately, no – I shall remain a bachelor – till you can assist me to that honour. (SIR HARCOURT *comes down – aside to* DAZZLE.) Keep the old boy away.

DAZZLE (*aside*). How do you get on?

YOUNG COURTLY (*aside*). Splendidly!

SIR HARCOURT. Is the conversation strictly confidential? – or might I join?

DAZZLE (*taking his arm*). Oh, not in the least, my dear sir – we were remarking that rifle shooting was an excellent diversion during the summer months.

SIR HARCOURT (*drawing himself up*). Sir, I was addressing –

DAZZLE. And I was saying what a pity it was I couldn't find anyone reasonable enough to back his opinion with long odds – come out on the lawn, and pitch up your hat, and I

---

[1] SIR HARCOURT *converses with* MAX.
[2] imbibed.
[3] *Insert:* MAX *leaves* SIR HARCOURT *and goes out to the balcony.*

will hold you ten to one I put a bullet into it every time, at forty paces.

SIR HARCOURT. No, sir – I consider you –

[MAX. Here, all of you – look, here is Lady Gay Spanker coming across the lawn at a hand gallop!

SIR HARCOURT (*running to the window*). Bless me, the horse is running away!

MAX. Look how she takes that fence! there's a seat.]

SIR HARCOURT. Lady Gay Spanker – who may she be?

GRACE. Lady Gay Spanker, Sir Harcourt? My cousin and dearest friend – you *must* like her.

SIR HARCOURT. It will be my devoir, since it is your wish – though it will be a hard task in your presence.

GRACE. I am sure she will like you.

SIR HARCOURT. Ha! ha! I flatter myself.

YOUNG COURTLY. Who, and what is she?

GRACE. Glee, glee made a living thing – Nature in some frolic mood shut up a merry devil in her eye, and, spiting Art, stole joy's brightest harmony to thrill her laugh, which peals out sorrow's knell. Her cry rings loudest in the field – the very echo loves it best, and, as each hill attempts to ape her voice, earth seems to laugh that it made a thing so glad.

MAX. Ay, the merriest minx I ever kissed.

LADY GAY *laughs without.*

LADY GAY (*without*). Max!

MAX. Come in, you mischievous puss.

*Enter* JAMES.

---

¹ (*A great whoop from* MAX.)

SIR HARCOURT. My God! what in heaven's name is that?

MAX. There she goes. Across the lawn at a hand gallop. Here, all of you. Look.

(*They all move to the window.*)

SIR HARCOURT. Bless me! The horse is running away.

DAZZLE. Who is it?

MAX. Lady Gay Spanker. Look how she takes that fence! There's a seat.

DAZZLE. Mind that gate. She's over.

JAMES. Mr Adolphus and Lady Gay Spanker.

*Enter* LADY GAY, *fully equipped in riding habit, etc.*

LADY GAY. Ha! ha! Well, Governor, how are ye? [I have been down five times, climbing up your stairs in my long clothes.] How are you, Grace, dear? (*Kisses her.*) There, don't fidget, Max. And there – (*Kisses him.*) – there's one for you.

SIR HARCOURT. Ahem!

LADY GAY. Oh, gracious, I didn't see you had visitors.

MAX. Permit me to introduce – Sir Harcourt Courtly, Lady Gay Spanker. Mr Dazzle, Mr Hamilton – Lady Gay Spanker.

SIR HARCOURT (*aside*). A devilish fine woman!

DAZZLE (*aside to* SIR HARCOURT). She's a devilish fine woman.

LADY GAY. You mustn't think anything of the liberties I take with [1][my old papa] here – bless him!

SIR HARCOURT. Oh, no! (*Aside.*) I only thought I should like to be in his place.

[2]LADY GAY. I am so glad you have come, Sir Harcourt. Now we shall be able to make a decent figure at the heels of a hunt.

SIR HARCOURT. Does your ladyship hunt?

LADY GAY. Ha! I say, Governor, does my ladyship hunt? I rather flatter myself that I do hunt! Why, Sir Harcourt, one might as well live without laughing as without hunting. Man was fashioned expressly to fit a horse. Are not hedges and ditches created for leaps? Of course! And I look upon foxes to be [one of] the most blessed dispensation[s] of a benign Providence.

SIR HARCOURT. Yes, it is all very well in the abstract: I tried it once.

LADY GAY. Once! Only once?

SIR HARCOURT. Once, only once. And then the animal ran away with me.

LADY GAY. Why, you would not have him walk!

SIR HARCOURT. Finding my society disagreeable, he instituted a series of kicks, with a view to removing the annoy-

---

[1] old grandad

[2] *Insert :* MEN (*turning chairs and offering them*). Lady Gay! ( *She chooses one and sits.*)

ance; but aided by the united stays of the mane and tail, I frustrated his intentions. His next resource, however, was more effectual, for he succeeded in rubbing me off against a tree.

MAX *and* LADY GAY. Ha! ha! ha!

DAZZLE. How absurd you must have looked with your legs and arms in the air, like a shipwrecked tea-table.

[1][SIR HARCOURT. I never looked absurd in my life. Ah, it

---

[1]SIR HARCOURT. Sir, I never looked absurd in my life. Ah, it may be very amusing in relation, I dare say, but very unpleasant in effect.

LADY GAY. I pity you, Sir Harcourt: it was criminal in your parents to neglect your education so shamefully.

SIR HARCOURT. Possibly; but be assured I shall never break my neck awkwardly from a horse, when it might be accomplished with less trouble from a bedroom window.

YOUNG COURTLY (*aside*). My dad will be run to ground by this huntress.

MAX (*to* SIR HARCOURT). You must leave your town habits in the smoke of London; here we rise with the lark.

SIR HARCOURT. Haven't the remotest conception when that is.

GRACE. The man that misses sunrise loses the sweetest part of the day.

SIR HARCOURT. Oh, pardon me; I have seen sunrise frequently after a ball, or from the window of my travelling carriage, and I always considered it disagreeable.

GRACE. I love to watch the first tear that glistens in the opening eye of morning, the silent song the flowers breathe, the thrilly choir of the woodland minstrels, to which the modest brook trickles applause; – these, swelling out the sweetest chord of sweet creation's matins, seem to pour some soft and merry tale into the daylight's ear, as if the waking world had dreamed a happy thing, and now smiled o'er the telling of it.

SIR HARCOURT. The effect of a rustic education! Who could ever discover music in a damp foggy morning, except those confounded waits, who never play in tune, and a miserable wretch who makes a point of crying coffee under my window just as I am persuading myself to sleep; in fact, I never heard any music worth listening to, except in Italy.

may be very amusing in relation, I dare say, but very unpleasant in effect.

LADY GAY. I pity you, Sir Harcourt: it was criminal in your parents to neglect your education so shamefully.

---

LADY GAY. No? then you never heard a well-trained English pack, full cry.

SIR HARCOURT. Full cry!

LADY GAY. Aye! there is harmony, if you will. Give me the trumpet-neigh; the spotted pack just catching scent. Their yelp – What a chorus! The view-hallo, blent with a peal of free and fearless mirth! That's our old English music, – match it where you can.

SIR HARCOURT (aside). I must see about Lady Gay Spanker.

DAZZLE (aside to SIR HARCOURT). Ah, would you –

MAX. Ah! Sir Harcourt, had you been here a month ago, you would have witnessed the most glorious run that ever swept over merry England's green cheek – a steeple-chase, sir, which I intended to win, but my horse threw me the day before. I had a chance, notwithstanding, and but for Gay here, I should have won. How I regretted my absence from it! How did my filly behave herself, Gay?

LADY GAY. Gloriously, Max! gloriously! There were sixty horses in the field, all mettle to the bone: the start was a picture – away we went in a cloud – pell-mell – helter-skelter – the fools first, as usual, using themselves up – we soon passed them – first your Kitty, then my Blueskin, and Craven's colt last. Then came the tug – Kitty skimmed the walls – Blueskin flew o'er the fences – the Colt neck and neck, and half a mile to run – at last the Colt baulked a leap and went wild. Kitty and I had it all to ourselves – she was three lengths ahead as we breasted the last wall, six feet, if an inch, and a ditch on the other side. Now, for the first time, I gave Blueskin his head – Ha! Ha! – Away he flew like a thunderbolt – over went the filly – I over the same spot, leaving Kitty in the ditch – walked the steeple, eight miles in thirty minutes, and scarcely turned a hair.

ALL. Bravo! Bravo!

LADY GAY. Do you hunt?

DAZZLE. Hunt! I belong to a hunting family. I was born on horseback and cradled in a kennel! Aye, and I hope I may die with a whoo-whoop!

SIR HARCOURT. Possibly; but be assured I shall never break my neck awkwardly from a horse, when it might be accomplished with less trouble from a bedroom window.

YOUNG COURTLY (*aside*). My dad will be caught by this she-Bucephalus tamer.

MAX. *Ah!* Sir Harcourt, had you been here a month ago, you would have witnessed the most glorious run that ever swept over merry England's green cheek – a steeple-chase, sir, which I intended to win, but my horse broke down the day before. I had a chance, notwithstanding, and but for Gay here, I should have won. How I regretted my absence from it! How did my filly behave herself, Gay?

LADY GAY. Gloriously, Max! gloriously! There were sixty horses in the field, all mettle to the bone: the start was a picture – away we went in a cloud – pell-mell – helter-skelter – the fools first, as usual, using themselves up – we soon passed them – first your Kitty, then my Blueskin, and Craven's colt last. Then came the tug – Kitty skimmed the walls – Blueskin flew o'er the fences – the Colt neck and neck, and half a mile to run – at last the Colt baulked a leap and went wild. Kitty and I had it all to ourselves – she was three lengths ahead as we breasted the last wall, six feet, if an inch, and a ditch on the other side. Now, for the first time, I gave Blueskin his head – Ha! Ha! – Away he flew like a thunderbolt – over went the filly – I over the same spot, leaving Kitty in the ditch – walked the steeple, eight miles in thirty minutes, and scarcely turned a hair.

ALL. Bravo! Bravo!

LADY GAY. Do you hunt?

DAZZLE. Hunt! I belong to a hunting family. I was born on horseback and cradled in a kennel! Aye, and I hope I may die with a whoo-whoop!]

MAX (*to* SIR HARCOURT). You must leave your town habits in the smoke of London; here we rise with the lark.

SIR HARCOURT. Haven't the remotest conception when that period is.

GRACE. The man that misses sunrise loses the sweetest part of his existence.

E

SIR HARCOURT. Oh, pardon me; I have seen sunrise frequently after a ball, or from the window of my travelling
carriage, and I always considered it disagreeable.

GRACE. I love to watch the first tear that glistens in the opening
eye of morning, the silent song the flowers breathe, the
thrilly choir of the woodland minstrels, to which the modest
brook trickles applause; – these, swelling out the sweetest
chord of sweet creation's matins, seem to pour some soft
and merry tale into the daylight's ear, as if the waking world
had dreamed a happy thing, and now smiled o'er the telling
of it.

SIR HARCOURT. The effect of a rustic education! Who could
ever discover music in a damp foggy morning, except
those confounded waits, who never play in tune, and a
miserable wretch who makes a point of crying coffee under
my window just as I am persuading myself to sleep; in
fact, I never heard any music worth listening to, except in
Italy.

LADY GAY. No? then you never heard a well-trained English
pack, full cry.

SIR HARCOURT. Full cry!

LADY GAY. Aye! there is harmony, if you will. Give me the
trumpet-neigh; the spotted pack just catching scent. What
a chorus in their yelp! The view-hallo, blent with a peal of
free and fearless mirth! That's our old English music, –
match it where you can.

SIR HARCOURT (aside). I must see about Lady Gay Spanker.

DAZZLE (aside to SIR HARCOURT). Ah, would you –

LADY GAY. [Time then appears as young as love, and plumes
as swift a wing.] Away we go! [The earth flies back to aid
our course!] Horse, man, hound, earth, heaven! – all – all –
one piece of glowing ecstasy! Then I love the world, myself,
and every living thing, – [1][a jocund soul cries out for very
glee, as it could wish that all creation had but one mouth that
I might kiss it!]

---

[1] – and I could wish that all creation had but one mouth that I
might kiss it!

SIR HARCOURT (*aside*). I wish I was the mouth!

MAX. Why, we will regenerate you, baronet.[1] But Gay, where is your husband? – Where is Adolphus!

LADY GAY. Bless me, where is my Dolly?

SIR HARCOURT. You are married, then?

LADY GAY. I have a husband somewhere, though I can't find him just now. Dolly, dear! (*Aside to* MAX.) Governor, at home I always whistle when I want him.

*Enter* SPANKER.

SPANKER. [Here I am,] – did you call me, Gay?

SIR HARCOURT (*eyeing him*). Is that your husband?

LADY GAY (*aside*). Yes, bless his stupid face, that's my Dolly.

MAX. Permit me to introduce you to Sir Harcourt Courtly.

SPANKER. How d'ye do? I – ah! – um! [2](*Appears frightened*.)]

LADY GAY. Delighted to have the honour of making the acquaintance of a gentleman so highly celebrated in the world of fashion.

SPANKER. Oh, yes, delighted, I'm sure – quite – very, so delighted – delighted!

[*Gets quite confused, draws on his glove, and tears it.*]

LADY GAY. Where have you been, Dolly?

SPANKER. Oh, ah, I was just outside.

MAX. Why did you not come in?

SPANKER. I'm sure I didn't – I don't exactly know, but I thought as – perhaps – I can't remember.

3

DAZZLE. Shall we have the pleasure of your company to dinner?

SPANKER. I always dine – usually – that is, unless Gay remains.

[4](LADY GAY. Stay dinner, of course; we came on purpose to stop three or four days.

---

[1] *Insert :* DAZZLE. Ay. We'll regenerate you.
    *He slaps* SIR HARCOURT *on the back.*
[2] (*He falls into a reverie.*)
[3] *Insert :* LADY GAY. He needs to put his feet up. He gets excited sitting in the carriage and watching me take the fences.
[4] LADY GAY. Stay dinner, of course; we came on purpose to stop three or four days, tell him.

GRACE. Will you excuse my absence, Gay?

MAX. What! what! Where are you going? What takes you away?

GRACE. We must postpone the dinner till Gay is dressed.

MAX. Oh, never mind, – stay where you are.

GRACE. No, I must go.

MAX. I say you shan't! I will be king in my own house.

GRACE. Do, my dear uncle; – you shall be king, and I'll be your prime minister, – that is, I will rule, and you shall have the honour of taking the consequences.

*Exit.*

LADY GAY. Well said, Grace; have your own way; it is the only thing we women ought to be allowed.

MAX. Come, Gay, dress for dinner.]

SIR HARCOURT. Permit me, Lady Gay Spanker.

LADY GAY. With pleasure, – what do you want?

[1][SIR HARCOURT. To escort you.

LADY GAY. Oh, never mind, I can escort myself, thank you, and Dolly too; – come, dear!]

*Exit.*

---

[1] SIR HARCOURT. To show you the way.

LADY GAY. Oh, I know the way, thank you.

MR SPANKER *does not reply.*

GRACE. Will you excuse my absence, uncle?

MAX. What! Where are you going? What takes you away?

GRACE. We must postpone dinner till Mr Spanker is rested.

MAX. Nonsense. I never saw a man so spry and eager.

GRACE. This way, Mr Spanker.

MAX. Hold your ground, Spanker. I will be king in my own house.

GRACE. And I'll be your prime minister. So I will rule and you shall have the honour of taking the consequences.

LADY GAY. Go with Grace, Dolly darling, and take your pumps off. I'll be along presently.

*Exeunt* SPANKER *and* GRACE.

MAX. Very well, ladies. Have your own way.

LADY GAY. If that's understood, I'll dress for dinner.

SIR HARCOURT. Au revoir!

[SPANKER. Ah, thank you!
    *Exit awkwardly*.]

SIR HARCOURT. What an ill-assorted pair!

MAX. Not a bit! She married him for freedom, and she has it; he married her for protection, and he has it.

SIR HARCOURT. How he ever summoned courage to propose to her, I can't guess.

MAX. [1][Bless you, he never did. She proposed to him! She says he would, if he could; but as he couldn't, she did for him.]
    *Exeunt, laughing*.
    *Enter* COOL *with a letter*.

COOL. Mr Charles, I have been watching to find you alone. Sir Harcourt has written [2][to town for you.]

YOUNG COURTLY. The devil he has!

COOL. He expects you[3][down] tomorrow evening.

DAZZLE. Oh! he'll be punctual. A thought strikes me.

YOUNG COURTLY. Pooh! Confound your thoughts! I can think of nothing but the idea of leaving Grace, at the very moment when I had established the most –

DAZZLE. What if I can prevent her marriage with your Governor?

YOUNG COURTLY. Impossible!

DAZZLE. He's pluming himself for the conquest of Lady Gay Spanker, It will not be difficult to make him believe she accedes to his suit. And if she would but join in the plan —

[4][YOUNG COURTLY. I see it all. And do you think she would?

DAZZLE. I mistake my game if she would not.]

COOL. Here comes Sir Harcourt!

DAZZLE. I'll begin with him. Retire, and watch how I'll open the campaign for you.

---

[1] Bless you, he didn't propose. She did. She said he would if he could; but, as he couldn't, she did it for him.

[2] to you in town.

[3] here

[4] YOUNG COURTLY. Oh no . . . Do you think she would?

DAZZLE. If she's the game bird I take her for – yes.

YOUNG COURTLY *and* COOL *retire.*
*Enter* SIR HARCOURT.

SIR HARCOURT. Here is that cursed fellow again.

DAZZLE. Ah, my dear old friend!

SIR HARCOURT. Mr Dazzle.

DAZZLE. I have a secret of importance to disclose to you. Are you a man of honour? Hush! don't speak; you are. It is with the greatest pain I am compelled to request you, as a gentleman, that you will shun studiously the society of Lady Gay Spanker!

SIR HARCOURT. Good gracious! [1][Wherefore, and by what right, do you make such a demand?]

DAZZLE. Why, I am distantly related to the Spankers.

SIR HARCOURT. Why, damme, sir, if you don't appear to be related to every family in Great Britain!

DAZZLE. A good many of the nobility claim me as a connection. But, to return – she is much struck with your address; evidently, she laid herself out for display.

SIR HARCOURT. Ha! you surprise me!

DAZZLE. To entangle you.

SIR HARCOURT. Ha! ha! why, it did appear like it.

DAZZLE. You will spare her for my sake; give her no encouragement; if disgrace come upon my relatives, the Spankers, I should never hold up my head again.

SIR HARCOURT (*aside*). I shall achieve an easy conquest, and a glorious. Ha! ha! I never remarked it before; but this is a gentleman.

DAZZLE. May I rely on your generosity?

SIR HARCOURT. Faithfully. (*Shakes his hand.*) Sir, I honour and esteem you; but, might I ask, how came you to meet our friend, Max Harkaway, in my house in Belgrave Square?

*Re-enter* YOUNG COURTLY. *Sits on sofa at back.*

DAZZLE. Certainly. I had an[2] [acceptance] of your son's for one hundred pounds.

SIR HARCOURT (*astonished*). Of my son's? Impossible!

---

[1] What's it to do with you?
[2] I. O. U.

DAZZLE. Ah, sir, fact! he paid a debt for a poor, unfortunate man – fifteen children – half-a-dozen wives – the devil knows what all.

SIR HARCOURT. Simple boy!

DAZZLE. Innocent youth, I have no doubt; when you have the hundred convenient, I shall feel delighted.

SIR HARCOURT. Oh! follow me to my room, and if you have the document, it will be happiness to me to pay it. Poor Charles! good heart!

DAZZLE. Oh, a splendid heart! I dare say. (*Exit* SIR HARCOURT.) [1][Come here; write me the bill.]

YOUNG COURTLY. What for?

DAZZLE. What for? why, to release the unfortunate man and his family, to be sure, from jail.

[2][YOUNG COURTLY. Who is he?

DAZZLE. Yourself.]

YOUNG COURTLY. But I haven't fifteen children!

DAZZLE. Will you take your oath of that?

YOUNG COURTLY. Nor four wives.

DAZZLE. More shame for you, with all that family. [Come, don't be obstinate;] write and date it back.

YOUNG COURTLY. [3][Ay, but where is the stamp?]

DAZZLE. Here they are [4][of all patterns.] (*Pulls out a pocket-book.*) I keep them ready drawn in case of necessity, [all but the date and acceptance.] Now, if you are in an autographic humour, you can try how your signature will look across half a dozen of them; – there – write – exactly – you know the place – across – good – and thank your lucky stars that you have found a friend at last, that gives you money and advice. (*Takes paper and exits.*)

YOUNG COURTLY. Things are approaching to a climax; I must

---

[1] Here, Charles. Bring your splendid heart here and sign your name.

[2] YOUNG COURTLY. Which man?

DAZZLE. You.

[3] Ay, but where are the I.O.U.s?

[4] for all amounts.

appear in *propria persona* – and immediately – but I must first ascertain what are the real sentiments of this riddle of a woman. Does she love me? I flatter myself. – [1][By Jove, here she comes – I shall never have such an opportunity again!]

*Enter* GRACE.

GRACE. I wish I had never seen Mr Hamilton. Why does every object appear robbed of the charm it once presented to me? Why do I shudder at the contemplation of this marriage, which, till now, was to me a subject of indifference? Am I in love? In love! – if I am, my past life has been the work of raising up a pedestal to place my own folly on – I – the infidel – the railer!

YOUNG COURTLY. Meditating upon matrimony, madam?

GRACE (*aside*). He little thinks he was the subject of my meditations! (*Aloud.*) No.

YOUNG COURTLY (*aside*). I must unmask my battery now.

GRACE (*aside*). How foolish I am – he will perceive that I tremble – I must appear at ease.

*A pause.*

YOUNG COURTLY. Eh! ah! um!

---

[1] And even if she does, ought I to pursue this affair further? My father's rival! As a dutiful son, I should feel concerned for his happiness; so I am. For I feel assured if Grace Harkaway becomes his bride he will for ever be miserable. It is therefore my duty as a loving son clearly to save my father. Yes, I'll be a sacrifice and marry her myself.

*Enter* PERT.

PERT. Oh, sir. It is agreed that Jenks and I shall go duet.

YOUNG COURTLY. Oh, really?

PERT. Yes, sir. For the dancing.

YOUNG COURTLY. Ah! Pert.

PERT. Yes, sir.

YOUNG COURTLY. Where's your mistress?

PERT. Taking her time, sir, descending.

YOUNG COURTLY. Alone, Pert?

PERT. Alone. (*Exit* PERT.)

YOUNG COURTLY. By Jove, I shall never have such an opportunity again!

GRACE. Ah! (*They sink into silence again. Aside.*) How very awkward.

YOUNG COURTLY (*aside*). It is a very difficult subject to begin. (*Aloud.*) Madam – ahem – there was – is – I mean – I was about to remark – a – (*Aside.*) Hang me if it is not a very slippery subject. I must brush up my faculties; attack her in her own way. (*Aloud.*) Sing! oh, muse. – (*Aside.*) Why, I have made love before to a hundred women!

GRACE (*aside*). I wish I had something to do, for I have nothing to say.

YOUNG COURTLY. Madam – there is – a subject so fraught with fate to my future life, that you must pardon my lack of delicacy, should a too hasty expression mar the fervent courtesy of its intent. To you I feel aware, I must appear in the light of a comparative stranger.

GRACE (*aside*). I know what's coming.

YOUNG COURTLY. Of you – I know perhaps too much for my own peace.

GRACE (*aside*). He *is* in love.

YOUNG COURTLY. I forget all that befell before I saw your beauteous self: I seem born into another world – my nature changed – the beams of that bright face falling on my soul, have, from its chaos, warmed into life the flowrets of affection, whose maiden odours now float towards the sun, pouring forth on their pure tongues a mite of adoration, midst the voices of a universe. (*Aside.*) That's something in her own style.

GRACE. Mr Hamilton!

YOUNG COURTLY. You cannot feel surprised –

GRACE. I am more than surprised. (*Aside.*) I am delighted.

YOUNG COURTLY. Do not speak so coldly.

GRACE. You have offended me.

YOUNG COURTLY. No, madam; no woman, whatever her state, can be offended by the adoration even of the meanest; it is myself whom I have offended and deceived – but still I ask your pardon.

GRACE (*aside*). Oh! he thinks I'm refusing him. (*Aloud.*) I am not exactly offended, but –

YOUNG COURTLY. Consider my position – a few days – and an insurmountable barrier would have placed you beyond my wildest hopes – you would have been my mother.

GRACE. I should have been your mother! (*Aside.*) I thought so.

YOUNG COURTLY. No – that is, I meant Sir Harcourt Courtly's bride.

GRACE (*with great emphasis*). Never!

YOUNG COURTLY. How! never! may I then hope? – you turn away – you would not lacerate me by a refusal?

GRACE (*aside*). How stupid he is!

YOUNG COURTLY. Still silent! I thank you, Miss Grace – I ought to have expected this – fool that I have been – one course alone remains – farewell!

GRACE (*aside*). Now he's going.

YOUNG COURTLY. Farewell forever! (*Sits.*) Will you not speak one word? I shall leave this house immediately – I shall not see you again.

GRACE. Unhand me, sir, I insist.

YOUNG COURTLY (*aside*). Oh! what an ass I've been! (*Rushes up to her, and seizes her hand.*) Release this hand? Never! never! (*Kissing it.*) Never will I quit this hand! it shall be my companion in misery – in solitude – when you are far way.

GRACE. Oh! should anyone come! (*Drops her handkerchief; he stoops to pick it up.*) For heaven's sake, do not kneel.

YOUNG COURTLY (*kneels*). Forever thus prostrate, before my soul's saint, I will lead a pious life of eternal adoration.

GRACE. Should we be discovered thus – pray, Mr Hamilton – pray – pray.

YOUNG COURTLY. Pray! I am praying; what more can I do?

GRACE. Your conduct is shameful.

YOUNG COURTLY. It is. (*Rises.*)

GRACE. And if I do not scream, it is not for your sake – that – but it might alarm the family.

YOUNG COURTLY. It might – it would. Say, am I wholly indifferent to you? I entreat one word – I implore you – do not withdraw your hand – (*She snatches it away – he puts his round her waist.*) – you smile.

GRACE. Leave me, dear Mr Hamilton!

YOUNG COURTLY. Dear! Then I am dear to you; that word once more; say – say you love me!

GRACE. Is this fair?

*He catches her in his arms, and kisses her.*

*Enter* LADY GAY SPANKER.

LADY GAY. Ha! oh!

GRACE. Gay! destruction!

*Exit.*

YOUNG COURTLY. Fizgig! The devil!

LADY GAY. Don't mind me – pray, don't let me be any interruption!

YOUNG COURTLY. I was just –

LADY GAY. Yes, I see you were.

YOUNG COURTLY. Oh! madam, how could you mar my bliss, in the very ecstasy of its fulfilment?

LADY GAY. I always like to be in at the death. Never drop your ears; bless you, she is only a little fresh – give her her head, and she will outrun herself.

YOUNG COURTLY. Possibly; but what am I to do?

LADY GAY. Keep your seat.

YOUNG COURTLY. But in a few days she will take a leap that must throw me – she marries Sir Harcourt Courtly.

LADY GAY. Why, that is awkward, certainly; but you can challenge him, and shoot him.

YOUNG COURTLY. Unfortunately, that is out of the question.

LADY GAY. How so?

YOUNG COURTLY. You will not betray a secret, if I inform you?

LADY GAY. All right – what is it?

YOUNG COURTLY. I am his son.

LADY GAY. What – his son? But does he not know you?

YOUNG COURTLY. No. I met him here, by chance, and faced it out. I never saw him before in my life.

LADY GAY. Beautiful! – I see it all – you're in love with your mother, that should be – your wife, that will be.

YOUNG COURTLY. Now, I think I could distance the old gentleman, if you will but lend us your assistance.

LADY GAY. I will, in anything.

YOUNG COURTLY. You must know, then, that my father, Sir Harcourt, has fallen desperately in love with you.

LADY GAY. With me! – (*Utters a scream of delight.*) – That is delicious!

YOUNG COURTLY. Now, if you only could –

LADY GAY. Could! – I will. Ha! ha! I see my cue. I'll cross his scent – I'll draw him after me. Ho! ho! won't I make love to him? Ha!

[1][YOUNG COURTLY. The only objection might be Mr Spanker, who might –

LADY GAY. No, he mightn't – he's no objection. Bless him, he's an inestimable little character – you don't know him as well as I do, I dare say – ha! ha! (*Dinner-bell rings.*) Here they come to dinner. I'll commence my operations on your Governor immediately! Ha! ha! how I shall enjoy it!]

YOUNG COURTLY. Be guarded!

    *Enter* MAX HARKAWAY, SIR HARCOURT, DAZZLE, GRACE, *and* SPANKER.

MAX. Now, gentlemen – Sir Harcourt, do you lead Grace.

LADY GAY. I believe Sir Harcourt is engaged to me. (*Takes his arm.*)

MAX. Well, please yourselves.

    *They file out,* MAX *first,* YOUNG COURTLY *and* GRACE, SIR HARCOURT *coquetting with* LADY GAY, *leaving* DAZZLE, *who offers his arm to* SPANKER.[2]

---

[1] *Dinner-bell rings.*

LADY GAY. Here they come to dinner. I'll commence my operations on your Governor immediately! Ha! Ha! How I shall enjoy it!

YOUNG COURTLY. The only objection might be Mr Spanker, who might –

LADY GAY. No, he mightn't – he's no objections. Bless him, he's an inestimable little character – you don't know him as well as I do, I dare say.

[2] *Insert:* INTERVAL.

# Act Four

## *SCENE ONE*

*A handsome drawing-room in Oak Hall, chandelier, tables with books, drawings, etc.*

> GRACE *and* LADY GAY *discovered.* [*Servant handing coffee.*]

GRACE. If there be one habit more abominable than another, it is that of the gentlemen sitting over their wine; it is a selfish, unfeeling fashion, and a gross insult to our sex.

LADY GAY. We are turned out just when the fun begins. [How happy the poor wretches look at the contemplation of being rid of us.]

GRACE. The conventional signal for the ladies to withdraw is anxiously and deliberately waited for.

LADY GAY. Then I begin to wish I were a man.

GRACE. The instant the door is closed upon us, there rises a roar!

LADY GAY. In celebration of their short-lived liberty, my love; rejoicing over their emancipation.

GRACE. I think it very insulting, whatever it may be.

LADY GAY. Ah! my dear, philosophers say that man is the creature of an hour – it is the dinner hour, I suppose.

> *Loud noise. Cries of 'A song, a song'.*

GRACE. I am afraid they are getting too pleasant to be agreeable.

LADY GAY. I hope the squire will restrict himself; after his third bottle, he becomes rather voluminous. (*Cries of 'Silence'.*) Someone is going to sing. (*Jumps up.*) Let us hear!

---

SPANKER *is heard to sing.*

GRACE. Oh no, Gay, for heaven's sake!

LADY GAY. Oho! ha! ha! why, that is my Dolly. (*At the conclusion of the verse.*) Well, I never heard my Dolly sing before!
[1][Happy wretches, how I envy them!]

*Enter* JAMES, *with a note.*

JAMES. Mr Hamilton has just left the house for London.

GRACE. Impossible! – that is, without seeing – that is –

LADY GAY. Ha! ha!

GRACE. He never – speak, sir!

JAMES. He left, Miss Grace, in a desperate hurry, and this note, I believe, for you. (*Presenting a note on a salver.*)

GRACE. For me!

*She is about to snatch it, but restraining herself, takes it coolly. Exit* JAMES.

[2]'Your manner during dinner has left me no alternative but instant departure; my absence will release you from the oppression which my society must necessarily inflict on your sensitive mind. It may tend also to smother, though it can never extinguish, that indomitable passion, of which I am the passive victim. Dare I supplicate pardon and oblivion for the past? It is the last request of the self-deceived, but still loving,

Augustus Hamilton.'

*Puts her hand to her forehead and appears giddy.*

LADY GAY. Hallo, Grace! [3]what's the matter?

GRACE (*recovering herself.*) Nothing – the heat of the room.[4]

LADY GAY. Oh! what excuse does he make? particular unforeseen business, I suppose?

GRACE. Why, yes – a mere formula – a – a – you may put it in the fire.

*She puts it in her bosom.*

---

[1] He never sings for me.

[2] *Insert:* GRACE, Excuse me, Gay.

LADY GAY. Certainly.

[3] *Insert:* Pull up;

[4] *Insert:* So very warm.

LADY GAY (*aside*). It is near enough to fire where it is.

GRACE. I'm glad he's gone.

LADY GAY. So am I.

GRACE. He was a disagreeable ignorant person.

LADY GAY. Yes; and so vulgar.

GRACE. No, he was not at all vulgar.

LADY GAY. I mean in appearance.

GRACE. Oh! how can you say so; he was [1][very] *distingué*.

LADY GAY. Well, I might have been mistaken, but I took him for a forward, intrusive –

GRACE. Good gracious, Gay! he was very retiring – even shy.

LADY GAY (*aside*). It's all right. *She* is in love, – blows hot and cold, in the same breath.

GRACE. How can you be a competent judge? Why, you have not known him more than a few hours, – while I – I –

LADY GAY. Have known him two days and a quarter! I yield – I confess, I never was, or will be, so intimate with him as you appeared to be! Ha! ha!

> [2][*Loud noise of argument. The folding-doors are thrown open.*]
>
> *Enter the whole party of gentlemen apparently engaged in warm discussion. They assemble in knots, while the servants hand coffee, etc.,* MAX, SIR HARCOURT, DAZZLE, *and* SPANKER, *together.*

DAZZLE. But, my dear sir, consider the position of the two countries under such a constitution.

SIR HARCOURT. The two countries! What have they to do with the subject?

MAX. Everything. Look at their two legislative bodies.

SPANKER. Ay, look at their two legislative bodies.

SIR HARCOURT. Why, it would inevitably establish universal anarchy and confusion.

GRACE. I think they are pretty well established already.

---

[1] excessively

[2] *The sound of the end of a rude story. The folding doors are thrown open. The conversation changes abruptly.*

SPANKER. Well, suppose it did, what has anarchy and confusion to do with the subject?

LADY GAY. Do look at my Dolly; he is arguing – talking
politics – 'pon my life he is. (*Calling.*) Mr Spanker, my dear!

SPANKER. Excuse me, love, I am discussing a point of importance.

LADY GAY. Oh, that is delicious; he must discuss that to me. –
(*She goes up and leads him down; he appears to have shaken
off his gaucherie; she shakes her head.*) Dolly! Dolly![1]

SPANKER. Pardon me, Lady Gay Spanker, I conceive your
mutilation of my sponsorial appellation derogatory to my
*amour propre*.

LADY GAY. Your what? Ho! ho!

SPANKER. And I particularly request that, for the future, I
may not be treated with that cavalier spirit which does not
become your sex, nor your station, your ladyship.

LADY GAY. [2][You have been indulging till you have lost the
little wit Nature dribbled into your unfortunate little head –
your brains want the whipper-in - you are not yourself.]

SPANKER. Madam, I am doubly myself; and permit me to
inform you, that unless you voluntarily pay obedience to my
commands, I shall enforce them.

LADY GAY. Your commands!

SPANKER. Yes, madam; I mean to put a full stop to your
hunting.

LADY GAY. You do! ah! (*Aside.*) [I can scarcely speak from
delight.] (*Aloud.*) [3][Who put such an idea into your head, for
I am sure it is not an original emanation of your genius?]

SPANKER. Sir Harcourt Courtly, my friend; and now, mark
me! I request, for your own sake, that I may not be compelled to assert my a – my authority, as your husband. I shall
say no more than this – if you persist in this absurd re-
bellion –

LADY GAY. Well?

---

[1] *Insert:* You've been imbibing.
[2] Go and put your feet up, Dolly. You're not yourself.
[3] Who put that idea into your head?

SPANKER. Contemplate a separation.

*He looks at her haughtily, and retires.*

LADY GAY. Now I'm happy! My own little darling, inestimable Dolly, has tumbled into a spirit, somehow. Sir Harcourt, too! Ha! ha! he's trying to make him ill-treat me, so that his own suit may thrive.

SIR HARCOURT (*advances*). Lady Gay!

LADY GAY (*aside*). Now for it.

SIR HARCOURT. What hours of misery were those I passed, when, by your secession, the room suffered a total eclipse.

LADY GAY. Ah! you flatter.

SIR HARCOURT. No, pardon me, that were impossible. No, believe me, I tried to join in the boisterous mirth, but my thoughts would desert to the drawing-room. Ah! how I envied the careless levity and cool indifference with which Mr Spanker enjoyed your absence.

DAZZLE (*who is lounging in a chair*). Max, that Madeira is worth its weight in gold; [1][I hope you have more of it.

MAX. A pipe, I think.

DAZZLE. I consider a magnum of that nectar, and a meerschaum of kanaster, to consummate the ultimatum of all mundane bliss. To drown myself in liquid ecstasy, and then blow a cloud on which the enfranchised soul could soar above Olympus. – Oh!]

*Enter* JAMES.

JAMES. Mr Charles Courtly!

SIR HARCOURT. Ah, now, Max, you must see a living apology for my conduct.

*Enter* YOUNG COURTLY, *dressed very plainly.*

Well, Charles, how are you? Don't be afraid. There, Max, what do you say now?

---

[1] How can you be so free with it?

MAX. At Oak Hall, sir, a guest is a guest.

DAZZLE. I consider a magnum of that nectar and a fragrant havana to be the summit of all mundane bliss. First drown yourself in liquid ecstasy, and then blow a cloud on which your expanding soul could soar above Olympus. – Oh.

MAX. Well, this is the most extraordinary likeness.

GRACE (*aside*). Yes – considering it is the original. I am not so easily deceived!

MAX. Sir, I am delighted to see you.

YOUNG COURTLY. Thank you, sir.

DAZZLE. Will you be kind enough to introduce me, Sir Harcourt?

SIR HARCOURT. This is Mr Dazzle, Charles.

YOUNG COURTLY. Which?

*Looking from* MR SPANKER *to* DAZZLE.

SIR HARCOURT (*to* LADY GAY). Is not that refreshing? Miss Harkaway – Charles, this is your mother, or rather will be.

YOUNG COURTLY. Madam, I shall love, honour, and obey you punctually. (*Takes out a book, sighs, and goes up reading.*)

[*Enter* JAMES.]

SIR HARCOURT. You perceive. Quite unused to society – perfectly ignorant of every conventional rule of life.

[1][JAMES. The Doctor and the young ladies have arrived.
   *Exit.*

MAX. The young ladies –] now we must to the ball – I make it a rule always to commence the festivities with a good old country dance – a rattling Sir Roger de Coverly; come, Sir Harcourt.

SIR HARCOURT. Does this antiquity require a war-whoop in it?

MAX. Nothing but a nimble foot and a light heart.

---

[1] *Enter* PERT.

PERT. Mr Jenks has arrived, sir, with his music.
   *Enter* JENKS *and his fiddle.*

MAX. Ladies and gentlemen, this is Jenks – full-time attorney and part-time fiddler.

PERT. The doctor and the young ladies are just taking their coats off.

MAX. Off you go, then.
   *Exeunt* PERT *and* JENKS.

[1][SIR HARCOURT. Very antediluvian indispensables! Lady
Gay Spanker, will you honour me by becoming my pre-
ceptor?

LADY GAY. Why, I am engaged –] but (*Aloud.*) on such a plea
as Sir Harcourt's, I must waive all obstacles.

MAX. Now, Grace, girl – give your hand to Mr Courtly.

GRACE. Pray, excuse me, uncle – I have a headache.

SIR HARCOURT (*aside*). Jealousy! by the gods. – Jealous of my
devotions at another's fame! (*Aloud.*) Charles, my boy!
amuse Miss Grace during our absence.

*Exit with* LADY GAY.

MAX. But don't you dance, Mr Courtly!

YOUNG COURTLY. Dance, sir! – I never dance – I [can
procure] exercise in a [much] more rational manner – and
music disturbs my meditations.

MAX. Well, do the gallant. [(*Exit.*)]

YOUNG COURTLY. I never studied that Art – but I have a
Prize Essay on a Hydrostatic subject, which would delight
her – for it enchanted the Reverend Doctor Pump, of
Corpus Christi.[2]

GRACE (*aside*). What on earth could have induced him to
disfigure himself in that frightful way! – I rather suspect
some plot to entrap me into a confession.

YOUNG COURTLY (*aside*). Dare I confess this trick to her?
No! Not until I have proved her affection indisputably. –
Let me see – I must concoct.

*He takes a chair, and, forgetting his assumed character, is
about to take his natural free manner.* GRACE *looks surprised. – He turns abashed.*

Madam, I have been desired to amuse you.

GRACE. Thank you.

YOUNG COURTLY. 'The labour we delight in, physics pain.'
I will draw you a moral, ahem! Subject, the effects of

---

[1]SIR HARCOURT. It sounds like a game of football! Lady Gay
Spanker, will you honour me by becoming my partner?
LADY GAY. Why, I am partnered already –
[2] *Insert: Exit* MAX, *nonplussed.*

inebriety! – which, according to Ben Johnson – means perplexion of the intellects, caused by imbibing spirituous liquors. – About an hour before my arrival, I passed an appalling evidence of the effects of this state – a carriage was overthrown – horses killed – gentleman in a hopeless state, with his neck broken – all occasioned by the intoxication of the post-boy.

GRACE. That is very amusing.

YOUNG COURTLY. I found it edifying – nutritious food for reflection – the expiring man desired his best compliments to you.

GRACE. To me –

YOUNG COURTLY. Yes.

GRACE. His name was –

YOUNG COURTLY. Mr Augustus Hamilton.

GRACE. Augustus! Oh! (*Affects to faint.*)

YOUNG COURTLY (*aside*). Huzza!

GRACE. But where, sir, did this happen?

YOUNG COURTLY. About four miles down the road.

GRACE. He must be conveyed here.

*Enter* SERVANT.

SERVANT. Mr Meddle, madam.

*Enter* MEDDLE.

MEDDLE. On very particular business.

GRACE. The very person. My dear sir!

MEDDLE. My dear madam![1]

GRACE. You must execute a very particular commission for me immediately. Mr Hamilton has met with a frightful accident on the London road, and is in a dying state.

MEDDLE. Well! I have no hesitation in saying, he takes it uncommonly easy – he looks as if he was used to it.

GRACE. You mistake: that is not Mr Hamilton, but Mr Courtly, who will explain everything, and conduct you to the spot.

YOUNG COURTLY (*aside*). Oh! I must put a stop to all this, or I shall be found out. – (*Aloud.*) Madam, that were useless;

---

[1] *Insert :* (*He hears the music.*) Jenks and his fiddle.
GRACE. Sir –

for I omitted to mention a small fact which occurred before I left Mr Hamilton – he died.

GRACE. Dear me! Oh, then we needn't trouble you, Mr Meddle. Hark! I hear they are commencing a waltz – if you will ask me – perhaps your society and conversation may tend to dispel the dreadful sensation you have aroused.

YOUNG COURTLY (*aside*). Hears of my death – screams out – and then asks me to waltz! I am bewildered! Can she suspect me? I wonder which she likes best – me or my double? Confound this disguise ! I must retain it – I have gone too far with my dad to pull up now. – At your service, madam.

GRACE (*aside*). I will pay him well for this trick!

*Exeunt.*

MEDDLE. [1][Well, if that is not Mr Hamilton, scratch me out with a big blade, for I am a blot – a mistake upon the rolls. There is an error in the pleadings somewhere, and I will discover it. – I would swear to his identity before the most discriminating jury. By the by, this accident will form a capital excuse for my presence here. I just stepped in to see how matters worked,] and – stay – here comes the bridegroom elect – and, oh! in his very arms, Lady Gay Spanker! (*Looks around.*) Where are my witnesses? Oh, that someone else were here! However, I can retire and get some information, eh – Spanker versus Courtly – damages – witness.

*Gets into an armchair, which he turns round.*

*Enter* SIR HARCOURT, *supporting* LADY GAY.

SIR HARCOURT. This cool room will recover you.

LADY GAY. Excuse my trusting to you for support.

SIR HARCOURT. I am transported! Allow me thus ever to

---

[1] Fiddle on, Jenks, for Rome is burning. Here's a Mr Charles Courtly, alias Hamilton and in the parlour of the Red Lion who should sit but a Mr Solomon Isaacs asking round the company if the name Mr Charles Courtly should be any way familiar. There's writs out for young Courtly. He's half-way to Newgate already. That information should be worth a guinea or two one way or another –

support this lovely burden, and I shall conceive that Paradise is regained.

*They sit.*

LADY GAY. Oh! Sir Harcourt, I feel very faint.

SIR HARCOURT. The waltz made you giddy.

LADY GAY. And I have left my salts in the other room.

SIR HARCOURT. I always carry a flacon, for the express accommodation of the fair sex. (*Producing a smelling-bottle.*)

LADY GAY. Thank you – ah! (*She sighs.*)

SIR HARCOURT. What a sigh was there!

LADY GAY. The vapour of consuming grief.

SIR HARCOURT. Grief? Is it possible, have you a grief? Are you unhappy? Dear me!

LADY GAY. Am I not married?

SIR HARCOURT. What a horrible state of existence!

LADY GAY. [1][I am never contradicted, so there are none of those enlivening, interesting little differences, which so pleasingly diversify the monotony of conjugal life, like spots of verdure – no quarrels, like oases in the desert of matrimony – no rows.]

SIR HARCOURT. How vulgar! what a brute!

LADY GAY. I never have anything but my own way; and he won't permit me to spend more than I like.

SIR HARCOURT. Mean-spirited wretch!

LADY GAY. How can I help being miserable?

SIR HARCOURT. Miserable? I wonder you are not in a lunatic asylum, with such unheard·of barbarism!

LADY GAY. But worse than all that!

SIR HARCOURT. [2][Can it be out-heroded?]

LADY GAY. Yes, I could forgive that – I do – it is my duty. But only imagine – picture to yourself, my dear Sir Harcourt, though I, the third daughter of an Earl, married him out of pity for his destitute and helpless situation as a bachelor with

----

[1] I am never contradicted, so there are none of those enlivening little differences to break the monotony of conjugal life like palm-trees in the desert – no rows.

[2] Can there be worse?

ten thousand a year – conceive, if you can – he actually permits me, with the most placid indifference, to flirt with any old fool I may meet.

SIR HARCOURT. Good gracious! miserable idiot!

LADY GAY. I fear there is an incompatibility of temper, which renders a separation inevitable.

SIR HARCOURT. Indispensable, my dear madam! Ah! had I been the happy possessor of such a realm of bliss – what a beatific eternity unfolds itself to my extending imagination! Had another man but looked at you, I should have annihilated him at once; [and if he had the temerity to speak, his life alone could have expiated his crime.]

LADY GAY. [1][Oh, an existence of such a nature is too bright for the eye of thought – too sweet to bear reflection.]

SIR HARCOURT. My devotion, eternal, deep –

LADY GAY. Oh, Sir Harcourt!

SIR HARCOURT (*more fervently*). Your every thought should be a separate study, – each wish forestalled by the quick apprehension of a kindred soul.

LADY GAY. Alas! how can I avoid my fate?

SIR HARCOURT. If a life – a heart – were offered to your astonished view by one who is considered the index of fashion – the [2][vane] of the *beau monde*, – if you saw him at your feet, begging, beseeching your acceptance of all, and more than this, what would your answer –

LADY GAY. Ah! I know of none so devoted!

SIR HARCOURT. You do! (*Throwing himself upon his knees.*) Behold Sir Harcourt Courtly!

MEDDLE *jumps up in the chair.*

LADY GAY (*aside*). Ha! ha! Yoicks! Puss has broken cover.

SIR HARCOURT. Speak, adored, dearest Lady Gay! – speak – will you fly from the tyranny, the wretched misery of such a monster's roof, and accept the soul which lives but in your presence!

LADY GAY. Do not press me. Oh, spare a weak, yielding

---

[1] Dear Sir Harcourt, do not tempt me with joys I have missed.
[2] pattern

woman, – be contented to know that you are, alas! too dear to me. But the world – the world would say –

SIR HARCOURT. [1][Let us be a precedent, to open a more extended and liberal view of matrimonial advantages to society.]

LADY GAY. How irresistible is your argument! [Oh! pause!]

SIR HARCOURT. [2][I have ascertained for a fact, every tradesman of mine lives with his wife, and thus you see it has become a vulgar and plebeian custom.]

LADY GAY. [3][Leave me;] I feel I cannot withstand your powers of persuasion. Swear that you will never forsake me.

SIR HARCOURT. Dictate the oath. May I grow wrinkled, – may two inches be added to the circumference of my waist, – may I lose the fall in my back, – may I be old and ugly the instant I forego one tithe of adoration!

LADY GAY. I must believe you.

SIR HARCOURT. Shall we leave this detestable spot – this horrible vicinity?

LADY GAY. The sooner the better; tomorrow evening let it be. Now let me return; my absence will be remarked. (*He kisses her hand.*) Do I appear confused? Has my agitation rendered me unfit to enter the room?

SIR HARCOURT. More angelic by a lovely tinge of heightened colour.

[4][LADY GAY. Tomorrow, in this room which opens on the lawn.

SIR HARCOURT. At eleven o'clock.]

LADY GAY. Have your carriage in waiting, and four horses. Remember please, be particular to have four; don't let the affair come off shabbily. Adieu, dear Sir Harcourt!

---

[1] Let us be a precedent to open up to society a more extended and liberal view of matrimony.

[2] Every tradesman lives with his wife. It has become a vulgar and plebeian custom.

[3] Oh pause!

[4] LADY GAY. Tomorrow night. Half-past eleven.
SIR HARCOURT. *Dans le jardin.*

*Exit.*

SIR HARCOURT. Veni, vidi, vici! Hannibal, Caesar, Napoleon, Alexander never completed so fair a conquest in so short a time. She dropped fascinated. This is an unprecedented example of the irresistible force of personal appearance combined with polished address. Poor creature! how she loves me! I pity so prostrating a passion, and ought to return it. I will; it is a duty I owe to society and fashion.

*Exit.*

MEDDLE (*turns the chair round*). 'There is a tide in the affairs of men, which taken in the flood, leads on to fortune.' [This is my tide – I am the only witness. 'Virtue is sure to find its own reward.' But] I've no time to contemplate what I shall be – something huge. Let me see – Spanker versus Courtly – Crim. Con. – Damages placed at 150,000 l., at least, for injuries always decimate your hopes.

*Enter* MR SPANKER.

SPANKER. I cannot find Gay anywhere.

MEDDLE. The plaintiff himself – I must commence the action. Mr Spanker, as I have information of deep, vital importance to impart, will you take a seat? (*They sit solemnly –* MEDDLE *takes out a note-book and pencil.*) Ahem! You have a wife?

*Re-enter* LADY GAY, *behind.*

SPANKER. Yes, I believe I –

MEDDLE. Will you be kind enough, without any prevarication, to answer my questions?

SPANKER. You alarm – I –

MEDDLE. Compose yourself and reserve your feelings; take time to consider. You have a wife?

SPANKER. Yes –

MEDDLE. He has a wife – good – a *bona-fide* wife – bound morally and legally to be your wife, and nobody else's in effect, except on your written permission –

SPANKER. But what has this –

MEDDLE. Hush! allow me, my dear sir, to congratulate you. (*Shakes his hand.*)

SPANKER. What for?

MEDDLE. Lady Gay Spanker is about to dishonour the bond of wedlock by eloping from you.

SPANKER (*starting*). What!

MEDDLE. [Be patient] – I thought you would be overjoyed. [1][Will you place the affair in my hands, and] I will venture to promise the largest damages on record.

SPANKER. Damn the damages! I want my wife. [Oh, I'll go and ask her not to run away. She may run away with me – she may hunt – she may ride – anything she likes.] Oh, sir, let us put a stop to this affair.

MEDDLE. Put a stop to it! do not alarm me, sir. Sir, you will spoil the most exquisite brief that was ever penned. [2][It must proceed – it shall proceed. It is illegal to prevent it, and I will bring an action against you for wilful intent to injure the profession.]

SPANKER. Oh, what an ass I am! Oh, I have driven her to this. It was all that damned brandy punch on the top of Burgundy. [What a fool I was!]

MEDDLE. It was the happiest moment of your life.

SPANKER. So I thought at the time; but we live to grow wiser. Tell me, who is the vile seducer?

MEDDLE. Sir Harcourt Courtly.

SPANKER. Ha! he is my best friend.

MEDDLE. I should think he is. If you will accompany me – here is a verbatim copy of the whole transaction in shorthand – sworn to by me.

SPANKER. Only let me have Gay back again.

MEDDLE. Even that may be arranged – this way.

SPANKER. That ever I should live to see my wife run away. Oh, I will do anything – keep two packs of hounds – buy up every horse and ass in England – myself included – oh!
*Exit with* MEDDLE.

LADY GAY. Ha! ha! ha! Poor Dolly, I'm sorry I must continue

---

[1] If you will place the affair in my hands

[2] It must proceed – it is illegal to prevent it. It shall proceed – or I will bring an action against you for wilful intent to injure the legal profession.

to deceive him. If he would but kindle up a little – so that fellow overheard all – well, so much the better.

*Enter* YOUNG COURTLY.

YOUNG COURTLY. My dear madam, how fares the plot? does my Governor nibble?

LADY GAY. Nibble! he is caught, and in the basket. I have just left him with a hook in his gills, panting for very lack of element. But how goes on your encounter?

YOUNG COURTLY. Bravely. By a simple ruse, I have discovered that she loves me. I see but one chance against the best termination I could hope.

LADY GAY. What is that?

YOUNG COURTLY. My father has told me that I return to town again tomorrow afternoon.

LADY GAY. Well, I insist you stop and dine – keep out of the way.

YOUNG COURTLY. Oh, but what excuse can I offer for disobedience? What can I say when he sees me before dinner?

LADY GAY. Say – say Grace.

*Enter* GRACE, *who gets behind the window curtains.*

YOUNG COURTLY. Ha! ha!

LADY GAY. I have arranged to elope with Sir Harcourt myself tomorrow night.

YOUNG COURTLY. The deuce you have!

LADY GAY. Now if you could persuade Grace to follow that example – his carriage will be waiting at the Park – be there a little before eleven – and it will just prevent our escape. Can you make her agree to that?

YOUNG COURTLY. Oh, without the slightest difficulty, if Mr Augustus Hamilton supplicates.

LADY GAY. Success attend you. (*Going.*)

YOUNG COURTLY. I will bend the haughty Grace. (*Going.*)

LADY GAY. Do.

*Exeunt severally.*

GRACE. Will you?

# ¹Act Five

## SCENE ONE

²[*A drawing-room in Oak Hall.*]

*Enter* COOL.

COOL. This is the most serious affair Sir Harcourt has ever been engaged in. I took the liberty of considering him a fool when he told me he was going to marry: but voluntarily to incur another man's incumbrance is very little short of madness. If he continues to conduct himself in this absurd manner, I shall be compelled to dismiss him.

*Enter* SIR HARCOURT, *equipped for travelling.*

SIR HARCOURT. Cool!

COOL. Sir Harcourt.

SIR HARCOURT. Is my chariot in waiting?

COOL. For the last half hour at the park wicket. But, pardon the insinuation, sir; would it not be more advisable to hesitate a little for a short reflection before you undertake the heavy responsibility of a woman?

SIR HARCOURT. No: hesitation destroys the romance of (a) *faux pas*, and reduces it to the level of a mere mercantile calculation.

COOL. What is to be done with Mr Charles?

SIR HARCOURT. [Ay, much against my will, Lady Gay prevailed on me to permit him to remain.] You, Cool, must return him to college. Pass through London, and deliver these papers: here is a small notice of the coming elopement for the *Morning Post*; this, by an eye-witness, for the *Herald*; this, with all the particulars, for the *Chronicle*; and the full

---

¹ ACT TWO, SCENE TWO.
² *11 p.m. the next night, outside Oak Hall.*

and circumstantial account for the evening journal – after which, meet us at Boulogne.

COOL. Very good, Sir Harcourt. (*Going.*)

SIR HARCOURT. Lose no time. Remember – Hotel Anglais, Boulogne-sur-Mer. And, Cool, bring a few copies with you, and don't forget to distribute some amongst very particular friends.

COOL. It shall be done. (*Exit* COOL.)

SIR HARCOURT. With what indifference does a man of the world view the approach of the most perilous catastrophe! [My position, hazardous as it is, entails none of that nervous excitement which a neophyte in the school of fashion would feel.] I am as cool and steady as possible. Habit, habit. [1][Oh! how many roses will fade upon the cheek of beauty, when the defalcation of Sir Harcourt Courtly is whispered – then hinted – at last, confirmed and bruited. I think I see them. Then, on my return, they will not dare to eject me – I am their sovereign! Whoever attempts to think of treason, I'll banish him from the West End – I'll cut him – I'll put him out of fashion!]

*Enter* LADY GAY.

LADY GAY. Sir Harcourt!

SIR HARCOURT. At your feet.

LADY GAY. I had hoped you would have repented.

SIR HARCOURT. Repented!

LADY GAY. Have you not come to say it was a jest? – say you have!

SIR HARCOURT. Love is too sacred a subject to be trifled with. Come, let us fly! See, I have procured disguises –

LADY GAY. My[2] courage begins to fail me. Let me return.

---

[1] Oh! how many roses will fade upon the cheek of beauty, when the defalcation of Sir Harcourt Courtly is hinted – then whispered – at last confirmed and bruited. I think I see them. Then, on my return, what awe, what power, what sovereignty. Let anyone think of treason – I'll cut him – I'll put him out of fashion – I'll banish him from the West End.

[2] *Insert* : SIR HARCOURT *produces two masks – the more decorative for himself.*

SIR HARCOURT. Impossible!

LADY GAY. Where do you intend to take me?

SIR HARCOURT. [1][You shall be my guide. The carriage waits.]

LADY GAY. You will never desert me?

SIR HARCOURT. Desert! Oh, heavens! Nay, do not hesitate – [flight, now, alone is left to your desperate situation! Come,] every moment is laden with danger. (*They are going.*)

LADY GAY. Oh! gracious!

SIR HARCOURT. Hush! what is it?

LADY GAY. I have forgotten – I must return.

SIR HARCOURT. Impossible!

LADY GAY. I must! I must! I have left Max – a pet stag-hound, in his basket – without whom, life would be unendurable – I could not exist!

SIR HARCOURT. No, no. Let him be sent after us in a hamper.

LADY GAY. In a hamper! Remorseless man! Go – you love me not. How would you like to be sent after me – in a hamper? Let me fetch him. Hark! I hear him squeal! Oh! Max – Max!

SIR HARCOURT. Hush! for heaven's sake. They'll imagine you're calling the Squire. [2][I hear footsteps; where can I retire?

---

[1] To the rainbow's end.

[2] MAX (*off*). Come, James. This way.

SIR HARCOURT. Voices. Discovered – unpleasant.

　　SIR HARCOURT *hides. Enter* MEDDLE, SPANKER, MAX, JAMES.

MEDDLE. Spanker versus Courtly. – I subpoena every one of you as witnesses! – I have 'em ready – here they are – shilling a-piece. (*Giving them round.*) I'll swear before any jury I overheard the whole elopement planned and now we stand witness to the execution.

MAX. But where is Sir Harcourt?

LADY GAY. Where is your defendant?

SPANKER. Aye. Where is your defendant?

MEDDLE. Mr Harkaway, do you seek Sir Harcourt and place a hand on his shoulder. The plaintiff and I will secure our affidavits.

*Enter* MEDDLE, SPANKER, DAZZLE *and* MAX. LADY GAY *screams.*

MEDDLE. Spanker versus Courtly! – I subpoena every one of you as witnesses! – I have 'em ready – here they are – shilling a-piece. (*Giving them round.*)

LADY GAY. Where is Sir Harcourt?

MEDDLE. There! – bear witness! – calling on the vile delinquent for protection!

SPANKER. Oh! his protection!

LADY GAY. What? ha!

MEDDLE. I'll swear I overheard the whole elopement planned – before any jury! – where's the book?

SPANKER. Do you hear, you profligate?

LADY GAY. Ha! ha! ha! ha!

DAZZLE. But where is this wretched Lothario?

MEDDLE. Aye, where is the defendant?

SPANKER. Where lies the hoary villain?

LADY GAY. What villain?

SPANKER. That will not serve you! – I'll not be blinded that way!

MEDDLE. We won't be blinded any way!

MAX. I must seek Sir Harcourt, and demand an explanation! – Such a thing never occurred in Oak Hall before! – It must be cleared up! (*Exit.*)

MEDDLE (*aside to* SPANKER). Now, take my advice, remember your gender. Mind the notes I have given you.]

SPANKER (*aside*). All right! Here they are! Now, madam, I have procured the highest legal opinion on this point.

MEDDLE. Hear! hear!

---

MAX. Down the long field, James.

JAMES *exits one way :* MAX *the other.* DAZZLE *enters, meeting* MAX.

MAX. Such a thing as this never occurred in Oak Hall before.

DAZZLE. What's afoot?

MAX. Villainy, sir. Villainy and rape.

DAZZLE. Oh, good.

     MEDDLE *urges* SPANKER *forward.*

MEDDLE. Now take my advice. Mind the notes I've given you and remember your gender.

SPANKER. And the question resolves itself into a – into – What's this? (*Looks at notes.*)

MEDDLE. A nutshell!

SPANKER. Yes, we are in a nutshell. [1][Will you, in every

---

[1] Will you unconditionally subscribe to this statement and respect my requests – desires – commands – (*Looks at notes.*) – orders – imperative – indicative – injunctive – or otherwise?

LADY GAY. 'Pon my life, he's actually going to assume the ribbons, and take the box-seat. I must put a stop to this. (*To* SPANKER.) Mr Spanker, I've been insulted by Sir Harcourt Courtly. He tried to elope with me. I place myself under your protection. Challenge him.

SPANKER. Ah! A challenge! I must consult my legal adviser.

SPANKER *and* MEDDLE *retire to consult.*

DAZZLE. Ah! I smell powder!

LADY GAY. It will all end in smoke. Sir Harcourt would rather run than fight.

DAZZLE (*loud*). My dear madam, command my services. Can I be of any use?

MEDDLE (*to* DAZZLE). On the subject of challenge, no – impossible.

DAZZLE. What has an attorney to do with affairs of honour? They are out of his element. Mr Spanker!

MEDDLE. Compromise the question! – pull his nose! – we have no objection to that.

DAZZLE (*turning to* Lady Gay). Well, we have no objection either – have we?

LADY GAY. No! – pull his nose – that will be something.

DAZZLE. Yes. Pull his nose.

SPANKER. But who's to do it?

MEDDLE. Exactly. And moreover it's not actionable.

DAZZLE. Isn't it? – thank you – I'll make use of that piece of information.

MEDDLE. Six and eightpence.

LADY GAY. Mr Spanker, I am determined! – I insist on a challenge being sent to Sir Harcourt Courtly! And – mark me – if you refuse to fight him – I will.

MEDDLE. Don't. Take my advice. You'll incapacitate yourself –

LADY GAY. Mr Meddle, hold your tongue. Mr Spanker!

DAZZLE. Mr Spanker!

respect, subscribe to my requests – desires – commands – (*Looks at notes.*) – orders – imperative – indicative – injunctive – or otherwise?

LADY GAY (*aside*). 'Pon my life, he's actually going to assume the ribbons, and take the box-seat. I must put a stop to this. I will! It will all end in smoke. I know Sir Harcourt would rather run than fight!

DAZZLE. Oh! I smell powder! – command my services. My dear madam, can I be of any use?

SPANKER. Oh! (a) challenge! – I must consult my legal adviser.

MEDDLE. No! – impossible!

DAZZLE. Pooh! the easiest thing in life! – Leave it to me – what has an attorney to do with affairs of honour? – they are out of his element!

MEDDLE. Compromise the question! – pull his nose! – we have no objection to that!

DAZZLE (*turning to* LADY GAY). Well, we have no objection either – have we?

LADY GAY. No! – pull his nose – that will be something.

MEDDLE. And, moreover, it is not exactly actionable!

DAZZLE. Isn't it! – thank you – I'll note down that piece of information – it may be useful.

MEDDLE. How! cheated out of my legal knowledge.

LADY GAY. Mr Spanker, I am determined! – I insist upon a challenge being sent to Sir Harcourt Courtly! – and – mark me – if you refuse to fight him – I will.

MEDDLE. Don't. Take my advice – you'll incapacit –

---

MEDDLE. Mr Spanker!

LADY GAY. Mr Meddle. Unless you wish me to horse-whip you, go home.

MEDDLE. That is assault and bestiality.

LADY GAY. Without witnesses it's rough justice.

    *They drive* MEDDLE *off.*

MEDDLE. You are thieves, vultures and ramping lions.

DAZZLE. Vanish, Meddle.

MEDDLE. And that is necromancy. (*Exit* MEDDLE.)

LADY GAY. Look you, Mr Meddle, unless you wish me to horsewhip you, hold your tongue.

MEDDLE. What a she-tiger – I shall retire and collect my costs. (*Exit.*)

LADY GAY. Mr Spanker, oblige me, by writing as I dictate.

SPANKER. He's gone – and now I am defenceless! Is this the fate of husbands? – A duel! – Is this the result of becoming master of my own family?

LADY GAY. 'Sir, the situation in which you were discovered with my wife, admits neither of explanation nor apology.'

SPANKER. Oh, yes! but it does – I don't believe you really intended to run quite away.

LADY GAY. You do not; but I know better, I say I did; and if it had not been for your unfortunate interruption, I do not know where I might have been by this time. – Go on.

SPANKER. 'Nor apology.' I'm writing my own death-warrant, committing suicide on compulsion.

LADY GAY. 'The bearer will arrange all preliminary matters for another day must see this sacrilege expiated by your life, or that of

> 'Yours very sincerely,
> 'DOLLY SPANKER.'

Now, Mr Dazzle. (*Gives it over his head.*)

DAZZLE. The document is as sacred as if it were a hundred-pound bill.

LADY GAY. We trust to your discretion.

SPANKER. His discretion! Oh, put your head in a tiger's mouth, and trust to his discretion!

DAZZLE (*sealing letter, etc., with* SPANKER'*s seal*). My dear Lady Gay, matters of this kind are indigenous to my nature, independently of their pervading fascination to all humanity; but this is more especially delightful, as you may perceive I shall be the intimate and bosom friend of both parties.

LADY GAY. Is it not the only alternative in such a case?]

DAZZLE. [1][It is a beautiful panacea in any, in every case. (*Going – returns.*) By the way,] where would you like this

---

[1] Now, sir.

party of pleasure to come off? Open-air shooting is pleasant enough, but if I might venture to advise, we could order half a dozen of that Madeira and a box of cigars into the billiard-room, so make a night of it;[1] take up the irons every now and then, string for first shot, and blaze away at one another in an amicable and gentlemanlike way; so conclude the matter before the potency of the liquor could disturb the individuality of the object, or the smoke of the cigars render its outline dubious. Does such an arrangement coincide with your views?

LADY GAY. Perfectly.

[2][DAZZLE. I trust shortly to be the harbinger of happy tidings. (*Exit.*)]

SPANKER (*coming forward*). Lady Gay Spanker, are you ambitious of becoming a widow?

LADY GAY. Why, Dolly, woman is at best but weak, and weeds become me.

[SPANKER. Female! am I to be immolated on the altar of your vanity?

LADY GAY. If you become pathetic. I shall laugh.]

SPANKER. Farewell – base, heartless, unfeeling woman! (*Exit.*)

LADY GAY. Ha! well, so I am. I am heartless, for he is a dear, good little fellow, and I ought not to play upon his feelings; but 'pon my life he sounds so well up at concert pitch, that I feel disinclined to untune him. Poor Dolly, I didn't think he cared so much about me. I will put him out of pain. (*Exit.*)

    SIR HARCOURT *comes down.*

SIR HARCOURT. I have been a fool! a dupe of my own vanity.

---

[1] *Insert :* Eh? Mr Spanker?

SPANKER. I don't smoke.

[2] DAZZLE. Then I'll pen you something sulphurous in the library. (*Exit.*)

SPANKER. I don't believe you really meant to run quite away.

LADY GAY. I say I did and, if it had not been for your unfortunate interruption, heaven knows where I might have been by this time. Follow Mr Dazzle, Dolly.

I shall be pointed at as a ridiculous old coxcomb – and so I am. [The hour of conviction is *arrived*.] Have I deceived myself? – Have I turned all my senses inwards – looking towards self – always self? – and has the world been ever laughing at me? Well, if they have, I will revert the joke; – they may say I am an old ass; but I will prove that I am neither too old to repent my folly, nor such an ass as to flinch from confessing it. A blow half met is but half felt.

*Enter* DAZZLE.

DAZZLE. Sir Harcourt, may I be permitted the honour of a few minutes' conversation with you?

SIR HARCOURT. With pleasure.

DAZZLE. Have the kindness to throw your eye over that. (*Gives the letter.*)

SIR HARCOURT (*reads*). 'Situation – my wife – apology – expiate – my life.' Why, this is intended for a challenge.

DAZZLE. Why, indeed, I am perfectly aware that it is not quite *en règle* in the couching, for with that I had nothing to do; but I trust that the irregularity of the composition will be confounded in the beauty of the subject.

SIR HARCOURT. Mr Dazzle, are you in earnest?

DAZZLE. Sir Harcourt Courtly, upon my honour I am, and I hope that no previous engagement will interfere with an immediate reply *in propria persona*. We have fixed upon the billiard-room as the scene of action, which I have just seen properly illuminated in honour of the occasion; and, by-the-by, if your implements are not handy, I can oblige you with a pair of the sweetest things you ever handled – hair-triggered – saw grip; heirlooms in my family. I regard them almost in the light of relations.

SIR HARCOURT. [Sir,] I shall avail myself of one of your relatives. [(*Aside.*) One of the hereditaments of my folly – I must accept it. (*Aloud.*)] Sir, I shall be happy to meet Mr Spanker at any time or place he may appoint.

DAZZLE. The sooner the better, sir. Allow me to offer you my arm. [1][I see you understand these matters; – my friend Spanker

---

[1] SIR HARCOURT *leaves, scorning* DAZZLE'S *arm.* DAZZLE *follows.*

is woefully ignorant – miserably uneducated. (*Exeunt –
re-enter* MAX, *with* GRACE).]

MAX. [1]Give ye joy, girl, give ye joy. Sir Harcourt Courtly must
consent to waive all title to your hand in favour of his son
Charles.

GRACE. Oh, indeed! Is that the pith of your congratulation –
humph! the exchange of an old fool for a young one?
Pardon me if I am not able to distinguish the advantage.

MAX. Advantage!

GRACE. Moreover, by what right am I a transferable cipher in
the family of Courtly? So, then, my fate is reduced to this,
to sacrifice my fortune, or unite myself with a worm-eaten
edition of the Classics!

MAX. Why, he certainly is not such a fellow as I could have
chosen for my little Grace; but consider, to retain fifteen
thousand a-year! Now, tell me honestly – [but why should I
say *honestly*? Speak, girl,] would you rather not have the lad?

GRACE. Why do you ask me?

MAX. Why, look ye, I'm an old fellow, another hunting season
or two, and I shall be in at my own death – I can't leave you
this house and land, because they are entailed, [nor can I say
I'm sorry for it, for it is a good law;] but I have a little box
with my Grace's name upon it, where, since your father's
death and miserly will, I have yearly placed a certain sum
to be yours, should you refuse to fulfil the conditions
prescribed.

GRACE. My own dear uncle! (*Clasping him round the neck.*)

MAX. Pooh! pooh! what's to do now? Why, it was only a
trifle – why, you little rogue, what are you crying about?

GRACE. Nothing, but –

MAX. But what? Come, out with it, will you have young
Courtly?

*Re-enter* LADY GAY.

LADY GAY. Oh! Max, Max!

MAX. Why, what's amiss with you?

---

[1] *Insert :* SCENE THREE
    *The interior of Oak Hall. Enter* MAX *and* GRACE.

LADY GAY. I'm a wicked woman!

MAX. What have you done?

LADY GAY. Everything – oh, I thought Sir Harcourt was a coward, but now I find a man may be a coxcomb without being a poltroon. Just to show my husband how inconvenient it is to hold the ribands sometimes, I made him send a challenge to the old fellow, and he, to my surprise, accepted it, and is going to blow my Dolly's brains out in the billiard-room.

MAX. The devil!

LADY GAY. Just when I imagined I had got my whip hand of him again, out comes my linch-pin – and over I go – oh!

[1][MAX. I will soon put a stop that – a duel under my roof!] Murder in Oak Hall! I'll shoot them both! (*Exit.*)

GRACE. Are you really in earnest?

LADY GAY. Do you think it like a joke? Oh! Dolly, if you allow yourself to be shot, I will never forgive you – never! Ah, he is a great fool, Grace; but I can't tell why, but I would sooner lose my bridle hand than he should be hurt on my account. [2][(*Enter* SIR HARCOURT COURTLY.)] Tell me – tell me – have you shot him – is he dead – my dear Sir Harcourt – you horrid old brute – have you killed him? I shall never forgive myself. (*Exit.*)

---

[1] MAX (*blows horn*). James! Wake up. James.

[2] *Insert :*

> *Enter* JAMES

JAMES. What's amiss, madam?

GRACE. The master needs you in the billiard-room.

> *Exit* JAMES.

MAX (*off*). Now come to your senses, do you hear? You may not duel under my roof.

> *Enter* PERT *and* JENKS *from upstairs, flurried.*

PERT. Is the house afire, Miss?

GRACE. No, Pert. Kindly fetch towels, bandages and . . . boil some hot water.

PERT (*looking at the weeping* LADY GAY). Madam!

> PERT *and* JENKS *out fast.*
>
> *Two shots from offstage.* GRACE *and* LADY GAY *hug each other and wait. The door opens. Enter* SIR HARCOURT.

GRACE. Oh! Sir Harcourt, what has happened?

SIR HARCOURT. Don't be alarmed, I beg – your uncle in-
terrupted us – discharged the weapons [1][– locked the
challenger up in the billiard-room to cool his rage.]

GRACE. Thank heaven![2]

SIR HARCOURT. Miss Grace, to apologize for my conduct

---

[1] out of the window.

[2] *Insert*:

    *Enter* MAX *with two smoking pistols.*

MAX. Out of my way, Sir Harcourt. I cannot bring myself to
speak to you.

    SIR HARCOURT *retires. The sound of a shoulder hurled
against a door offstage.*

(*To* GRACE.) I locked the challenger in the library to restore his
equilibrium.

    *Enter* PERT *and* JENKS *with water and first aid.*

GRACE. Thank you, Pert. It is not necessary.

    *They withdraw. Enter* JAMES.

JAMES. I'm not sure the woodwork will stand it, sir. He be
coming at it like the Spanish Armada.

    *The sound of splintering wood.* SPANKER *is propelled on-
stage.*

SPANKER. By what right, sir, do you interrupt a gentleman's
moment? My good friend Courtly was braced. I was braced.
You, sir, are an old maggot.

MAX. James, take this he-tiger out into the night air to cool his
rage.

SPANKER. I AM NOT ANGRY.

    SPANKER *faints rigid with anger.* JAMES *carries him off.
Enter* DAZZLE.

DAZZLE. Max, you have your finger on my trigger.

    DAZZLE *takes the pistols from* MAX *and exits.*

    GRACE *and* MAX *sit down to draw breath.* SIR HARCOURT
*moves a step towards them.*

GRACE. Uncle.

MAX. Sir Harcourt.

SIR HARCOURT. May I be allowed a word alone with Miss
Grace?

MAX. Certainly. Why not? Certainly.

    *Exit* MAX.

were useless, more especially as I am confident that no feelings of indignation or sorrow for my late acts are cherished by you; but still, reparation is in my power, and I not only waive all title, right, or claim to your person or your fortune, but freely admit your power to bestow them on a more worthy object.

GRACE. This generosity, Sir Harcourt, is most unexpected.

SIR HARCOURT. No, not generosity, but simply justice, justice!

GRACE. May I still beg a favour?

SIR HARCOURT. Claim anything that is mine to grant.

GRACE. You have been duped by Lady Gay Spanker, I have also been cheated and played upon by her and Mr Hamilton – may I beg that the contract between us may, to all appearances, be still held good?

SIR HARCOURT. Certainly, although I confess I cannot see the point of your purpose.

*Enter* MAX, *with* YOUNG COURTLY.

MAX. Now, Grace, I have brought the lad.

GRACE. Thank you, uncle, but the trouble was quite unnecessary – Sir Harcourt holds to his original contract.

MAX. The deuce he does!

GRACE. And I am willing – nay, eager to become Lady Courtly.

YOUNG COURTLY (*aside*). The deuce you are!

MAX. But, Sir Harcourt –

SIR HARCOURT. One word, Max, for an instant. (*They retire.*)

YOUNG COURTLY (*aside*). What can this mean? Can it be possible that I have been mistaken – that she is not in love with Augustus Hamilton?

GRACE. Now we shall find how he intends to bend the haughty Grace.

YOUNG COURTLY. Madam – Miss, I mean – are you really in earnest – are you in love with my father?

GRACE. No, indeed I am not.

YOUNG COURTLY. Are you in love with anyone else?

GRACE. No, or I should not marry him.

YOUNG COURTLY. Then you actually accept him as your real husband?

GRACE. In the common acceptation of the word.

YOUNG COURTLY (*aside*). Hang me if I have not been a pretty fool! (*Aloud.*) Why do you marry him, if you don't care about him?

GRACE. To save my fortune.

YOUNG COURTLY (*aside*). Mercenary, cold-hearted girl! (*Aloud.*) [But if there be anyone you love in the least – marry him;] – were you never in love?

GRACE. Never!

YOUNG COURTLY (*aside*). Oh! what an ass I've been! (*Aloud.*) I heard Lady Gay mention something about a Mr Hamilton.

GRACE. Ah, yes, a person who, after an acquaintanceship of two days, had the assurance to make love to me, and I –

YOUNG COURTLY. Yes, – you – Well?

GRACE. I pretended to receive his attentions.

YOUNG COURTLY (*aside*). It was the best pretence I ever saw.

[GRACE. An absurd, vain, conceited coxcomb, who appeared to imagine that I was so struck with his fulsome speech, that he could turn me round his finger.

YOUNG COURTLY (*aside*). My very thoughts!

GRACE. But he was mistaken.

YOUNG COURTLY (*aside*). Confoundedly! (*Aloud.*)] Yet you seemed rather concerned about the news of his death?

GRACE. His accident! No, but –

YOUNG COURTLY. But what?

GRACE (*aside*). What can I say? (*Aloud.*) Ah! but my maid Pert's brother is a post-boy, and I thought he might have sustained an injury, poor boy.

YOUNG COURTLY (*aside*). Damn the post-boy! (*Aloud.*) Madam, if the retention of your fortune be the plea on which you are about to bestow your hand on one you do not love, and whose very actions speak his carelessness for that inestimable jewel he is incapable of appreciating – Know that I am devotedly, madly attached to you.

GRACE. You, sir? Impossible!

YOUNG COURTLY. Not at all, – [but inevitable,] – I have been
so for a long time.

GRACE. Why, you never saw me until last night.

YOUNG COURTLY. I have seen you in imagination – you are
the ideal I have worshipped.

GRACE. Since you press me into a confession, – which nothing
but this could bring me to speak, – know, I did love poor
Augustus Hamilton – (MAX *and* SIR HARCOURT *re-enter.*)
but he – he is – no – more! Pray, spare me, sir.

YOUNG COURTLY (*aside*). She loves me! And oh! what a
situation I am in! – if I own I am the man, my Governor will
overhear, and ruin me – if I do not, she'll marry him. – What
is to be done?

   *Enter* LADY GAY.

LADY GAY. Where have you put my Dolly? I have been racing
all round the house – tell me, is he quite dead!

MAX. I'll have him brought in. (*Exit.*)

SIR HARCOURT. My dear madam, you must perceive this
unfortunate occurrence was no fault of mine. I was compelled to act as I have done – I was willing to offer any
apology, [but that resource was excluded, as unacceptable.]

LADY GAY. I know – I know – ['twas I made him write that
letter] – there was no apology required – 'twas I that
apparently seduced you from the paths of propriety – 'twas
all a joke, and here is the end of it. (*Enter* MAX, MR SPANKER,
*and* DAZZLE[1].) Oh! if he had but lived to say, 'I forgive you,
Gay!'

SPANKER. So I do!

LADY GAY (*seeing* SPANKER). Ah! he is alive!

SPANKER. Of course I am!

LADY GAY. Ha! ha! ha! (*Embraces him.*) I will never hunt
again – unless you wish it. Sell your stable –

SPANKER. No, no – do what you like – say what you like, for
the future! [I find the head of a family has less ease and more
responsibility than I, as a member, could have anticipated.
I abdicate!]

---

[1] *Insert :* PERT *and* JENKS *follow.*

*Enter* COOL.

SIR HARCOURT. Ah! Cool, here! (*Aside.*) You may destroy those papers – I have altered my mind, – and I do not intend to elope at present. Where are they?

COOL. As you seemed particular, Sir Harcourt, I sent them off by mail to London.

SIR HARCOURT. Why, then a full description of the whole affair will be published tomorrow.

COOL. Most irretrievably?

SIR HARCOURT. You must post to town immediately, and stop the press.

COOL. Beg pardon – they would see me hanged first, Sir Harcourt; they don't frequently meet with such a profitable lie.

[1][SERVANT (*without*). No, sir! no, sir!

*Enter* SIMPSON.

SIMPSON. Sir, there is a gentleman, who calls himself Mr Solomon Isaacs, insists upon following me up.

*Enter* MR SOLOMON ISAACS.

ISAACS. Mr Courtly, you will excuse my performance of a most disagreeable duty at any time, but more especially in such a manner. I must beg the honour of your company to town.

SIR HARCOURT. What! – how! – what for?

---

[1] JAMES (*without*). No, sir! no, sir!

*Enter* MEDDLE *at speed followed by* ISAACS *and* JAMES.

MEDDLE. Would have been in sooner but a pellet through my hat encouraged us to lie low in the bushes till the firing ceased. And that's a thing to be looked into. But currently – my client, Mr Isaacs has a word or two to say.

ISAACS. Mr Courtly, you will excuse my performance of a most disagreeable duty. I must beg the honour of your company to town.

MEDDLE. To town.

SIR HARCOURT. What! – How? – what for?

ISSACS. For debt, Sir Harcourt.

MEDDLE. Debt.

SIR HARCOURT. Debt?

ISAACS. For debt, Sir Harcourt.

SIR HARCOURT. Arrested?] – impossible! Here must be some mistake.

ISAACS. Not the slightest, sir. Judgment has been given in five cases, for the last three months; but Mr Courtly is an eel, rather too nimble for my men. – We have been on his track, and traced him down to this village, with Mr Dazzle.

DAZZLE. Ah! Isaacs! how are you?

[ISAACS. Thank you, sir. (*Speaks to* SIR HARCOURT.)]

MAX. Do you know him?

DAZZLE. Oh, intimately – distantly related to his family – same arms on our escutcheon – empty purse falling through a hole in a – pocket: [motto, 'Requiescat in pace' – which means, 'Let virtue be its own reward.']

SIR HARCOURT (*to* ISAACS). Oh, I thought there was a mistake! Know, to your misfortune, that Mr Hamilton was the person you dogged to Oak Hall, between whom and my son a most remarkable likeness exists.

ISAACS. Ha! ha! Know, to your misfortune, Sir Harcourt, that Mr Hamilton and Mr Courtly are one and the same person!

SIR HARCOURT. Charles!

YOUNG COURTLY. Concealment is in vain – I am Augustus Hamilton.

[SIR HARCOURT. Hang me, if I didn't think it all along! Oh, you infernal, cozening dog!

---

[1] ISAACS. Very well, thank you, sir.

  ISAACS *and* MEDDLE *talk privately with* SIR HARCOURT.

[2] SIR HARCOURT. Hang me if I didn't think it all along! You're no son of mine!

YOUNG COURTLY (*turning to* MEDDLE *and* ISAACS). Gentlemen!

  *He surrenders himself. They start to exit.*

GRACE. Stay, sir – Mr Charles Courtly is under age – ask his father.

  CHARLES *returns.*

SIR HARCOURT. Ahem! – I won't – I won't pay a shilling of the rascal's debts – not a sixpence!

  YOUNG COURTLY *and his captors start to exit again.*

ISAACS. Now, then, Mr Hamilton –

GRACE. Stay, sir – Mr Charles Courtly is under age – ask his father.

SIR HARCOURT. Ahem! – I won't – I won't pay a shilling of the rascal's debts – not a sixpence!

GRACE. Then, I will – you may retire.

   *Exit* ISAACS.]

YOUNG COURTLY. I can now perceive the generous point of your conduct towards me; and, believe me, I appreciate, and will endeavour to deserve it.

MAX. Ha! ha! Come, Sir Harcourt, you have been fairly beaten – you must forgive him – say you will.

SIR HARCOURT. So, sir, it appears you have been leading, covertly, an infernal town life.

YOUNG COURTLY. Yes, [please,] father. [(*Imitating* MASTER CHARLES.)

SIR HARCOURT. None of your humbug, sir! (*Aside.*) He is my own son – how could I expect him to keep out of the fire? (*Aloud.*)] And you, Mr Cool! – have you been deceiving me?

COOL. Oh! Sir Harcourt, if your perception was played upon, how could I be expected to see?[1]

---

[1] *Insert :* straight.

---

GRACE. Then I will.

YOUNG COURTLY. Madam!

MAX. Jenks! You're the only entirely wordless lawyer I've encountered – accompany Mr Isaacs to the library and see him well settled.

MEDDLE (*moving in on* JENKS). Jenks? Jenks? Why he's a jumped-up fiddler with as much knowledge of the law as a pat of butter.

PERT (*cornering* MEDDLE). Would you repeat that, Mr Meddle? Slowly?

MEDDLE (*defeated suddenly*). Oh damn . . . I know . . . (*Sniggers.*) Slander.

   MEDDLE *makes an accelerating exit.*

GRACE (*to* ISAACS). Follow Mr Jenks, sir.

ISAACS. Thank you, madam.

   PERT *and* JENKS *lead* ISAACS *away.*

SIR HARCOURT. Well, it would be useless to withhold my hand. There, boy! (*He gives his hand to* YOUNG COURTLY. GRACE *comes down on the other side, and offers her hand; he takes it.*) What is all this? What do you want?

YOUNG COURTLY. Your blessing, father.

GRACE. If you please, father.

SIR HARCOURT. Oho! the mystery is being solved. So, so, you young scoundrel, you have been making love – under the rose.

LADY GAY. He learnt that from you, Sir Harcourt.

SIR HARCOURT. Ahem! What would you do now, if I were to withhold my consent?

GRACE. *Do* without it.

MAX. The will says, if Grace marries anyone but you, – her property reverts to your heir-apparent – and there he stands.

LADY GAY. Make a virtue of necessity.

SPANKER. I married from inclination; and see how happy I am. And if ever I have a son –

LADY GAY. Hush! Dolly, dear!

SIR HARCOURT. Well! take her, boy! Although you are too young to marry. (*They retire with* MAX.)

LADY GAY. Am I forgiven, Sir Harcourt?

SIR HARCOURT. Ahem! Why – a – (*Aside.*) Have you really deceived me?

LADY GAY. Can you not see through this?

SIR HARCOURT. And you still love me?

LADY GAY. As much as I ever did.

SIR HARCOURT (*is about to kiss her hand, when* SPANKER *interposes between*). A very handsome ring, indeed.

SPANKER. Very. (*Puts her arm in his, and they go up.*)

SIR HARCOURT. Poor little Spanker!

MAX (*coming down, aside to* SIR HARCOURT). One point I wish to have settled. Who is Mr Dazzle!

SIR HARCOURT. A relative of the Spankers, he told me.

MAX. Oh, no, – near connection of yours.

SIR HARCOURT. Never saw him before I came down here, in all my life. (*To* YOUNG COURTLY.) Charles, who is Mr Dazzle?

YOUNG COURTLY. Dazzle, Dazzle, – will you excuse an impertinent question? – but who the deuce are you?

DAZZLE. Certainly. I have not the remotest idea!

ALL. How, sir?

DAZZLE. Simple question as you may think it, it would puzzle half the world to answer. One thing I can vouch – Nature made me a gentleman – that is, I live on the best that can be procured for credit. I never spend my own money when I can oblige a friend. I'm always thick on the winning horse. I'm an epidemic on the trade of tailor. For further particulars, inquire of any sitting magistrate.

SIR HARCOURT. And these are the deeds which attest your title to the name of gentleman? I perceive that you have caught the infection of the present age. Charles, permit me, as your father, and you, sir, as his friend, to correct you on one point. Bare-faced assurance is the vulgar substitute for gentlemanly ease; and there are many who, by aping the *vices* of the great, imagine that they elevate themselves to the rank of those whose faults alone they copy. No, sir! The title of gentleman is the only one *out* of any monarch's gift, yet within the reach of every peasant. It should be engrossed by *Truth* – stamped with *Honour* – sealed with *good-feeling* – signed *Man* – and enrolled in every true young English heart.

CURTAIN